Conglomerate Rock

Conglomerate Rock

The Music Industry's Quest to Divide Music and Conquer Wallets

David J. Park

LEXINGTON BOOKS

A division of
ROWMAN & LITTLEFIELD PUBLISHERS, INC.
Lanham • Boulder • New York • Toronto • Plymouth, UK

LEXINGTON BOOKS

A division of Rowman & Littlefield Publishers, Inc.
A wholly owned subsidiary of The Rowman & Littlefield Publishing Group, Inc.
4501 Forbes Boulevard, Suite 200
Lanham, MD 20706

Estover Road
Plymouth PL6 7PY
United Kingdom

British Library Cataloguing in Publication Information Available

Library of Congress Cataloging-in-Publication Data

Park, David J.
  Conglomerate rock : the music industry's quest to divide music and conquer wallets /
David J. Park.
    p. cm.
  Includes bibliographical references and index (p.   ).
  ISBN 978-0-7391-1501-5

  1. Music trade. 2. Music and the Internet—Economic aspects. I. Title.
  ML3790.P345 2007
  381'.4578—dc22

                                                                    2007006816

Printed in the United States of America

♾™ The paper used in this publication meets the minimum requirements of American
National Standard for Information Sciences—Permanence of Paper for Printed Library
Materials, ANSI/NISO Z39.48–1992.

Contents

Charts and Graphs

Charts

Graphs

Acknowledgements

I need to thank Doug McLeod at the University of Wisconsin for his support, guidance and constructive feedback. I would also like to thank Gay Seidman, Dhavan Shah, Rob Howard and Michelle Nelson. Their words of wisdom have been helpful during the time I researched and wrote this book. I also want to thank everyone at the University of Wisconsin-Madison School of Journalism and Mass Communication. They were extremely kind for taking me in as a homeless hurricane evacuee right after the levees breached New Orleans in 2005. Not only did they provide me with office space and resources during the fall semester, but they also provided me with much needed friendship, counsel and understanding. The wonderful and generous Susie Brandscheid, Atsushi Tajima and Sandy Nichols also deserve praise for organizing support for me, as do all of my other friends and colleagues who helped in my time of need. I can only hope to repay you one day with the same generosity you were kind enough to extend to me.

Gi Woong Yun at Bowling Green State University, Sameer Deshpande at the University Lethbridge (Canada), Atsushi Tajima at the University of Wisconsin-Madison and Dr. Aloke Thakore were also kind enough to offer feedback on earlier drafts. In addition, I also owe special thanks to Bob McChesney, Jack Mitchell and Siva Vaidhyanathan for their inspiration, good humor and counsel. Please attribute the strengths in this book to the people mentioned here and hold me responsible for any flaws. I would also like to thank the Howard Hughes Medical Institute for some financial assistance during the fall of 2005.

Finally, one cannot finish a book without thanking his or her family and friends for their encouragement and support. I am grateful to my parents for their love, support and confidence in me. They are truly wonderful people who have not only devoted their lives to education, but also to being kind, generous and humble. My friends Laura Miles, Steve Wade and Paul Harding also deserve special praise for providing additional support and valued conversations. This book is dedicated to the people who lost their lives and livelihoods as a result of the levee breach in New Orleans.

CHAPTER 1

MUSIC INDUSTRY IN TRANSITION

"Technology has destabilized us, it has hurt us . . . but now it's going to take us to new heights."
— Doug Morris, Chief Executive of Vivendi's Universal Music Group (Harmon, 2003e)

This book argues that access to music is becoming more dispersed, expensive and difficult to acquire, while at the same time it is becoming easier to see and hear artists from a handful of transnational corporations in commercial culture. The music industry is dividing access to new releases through different subscription services, hardware and new media like audio DVDs in hopes of conquering consumers' wallets and purses. Music for pay now requires different service fees and additional hardware for access, while music for promotion is freely spread throughout the media. Even while this is happening consumers are still able to find free music on file sharing services such as Kazaa, although they now risk fines and jail time for doing so. While an extremely consolidated and conglomerated music industry is driving these changes, its development and use of technology is at the heart of this discussion. The industry's use of technology and its legal efforts to regulate it appear to be having powerful effects on access to music and culture.

The remaining pages present a critical analysis of trends and technology in the music industry aimed at provoking public discussion concerning the interaction between industry practice and music consumption. It is a recent history covering a period from roughly 1999–2005. This period is important because it

1

signifies the beginning of the music industry's transition into the digital sphere with its use of the Internet, as well as recent restructuring given the industry's first significant sales decline in twenty years. Because the industry is constantly changing and rarely static, this is a work in progress needing to be updated. Some music industry related companies are likely to have merged, separated, or developed differently by the time this book is published. Nonetheless, the strategies developed by the industry described during this period will have long-term effects concerning the way consumers experience and access music, as well as how culture is viewed and portrayed in the United States and increasingly throughout the world.

As this book highlights the importance of access to music, it would be a travesty if it was not accessible to a broad range of people. Therefore, it is hoped this book will appeal to students, scholars, musicians, policy makers and music fans. Students may find the content useful concerning the commercialization and creation of the music they listen to on their iPods and computers. Consumers and musicians may find the often invisible production processes interesting, while policy makers will find evidence in order to regulate the industry in favor of a more democratic and accessible culture.

CONTEXT

The music industry is in a state of structural transition. It is changing its long-term business and marketing strategies as a result of at least two recent developments. First is the invention of the Internet, and second is the recent decline in global music sales. The Internet is enabling the music industry to by-pass traditional retail stores and sell digital music files directly to consumers. Because of this technology, the industry now saves on distribution, transportation, postage, and storage costs. The major labels are also creating a digital distribution system better suited to their needs through additional measures designed to protect copyright. In fact, the major labels now spy on and track consumer behavior related to music consumption. Even though the music industry stands to gain more than it may lose in the transition to the online world, the Internet also has potential to challenge the major labels' control and dominance of global music distribution. File sharing sites such as Kazaa, eDonkey, and others are challenging traditional modes of consumption and distribution by providing Internet users with the ability to share music for free. The Internet may also hold potential to empower independent musicians and consumers so they no longer have to work with major labels.

The music industry argues the results of these challenges have been driving global music sales downward. Indeed, for the first time in nearly two decades, global music sales have been in decline (Koehn 2003). Although there are several factors associated with sales declines, such as the industry's elimination of CD singles, the end of the CD replacement cycle (where consumers replaced their vinyl albums with CDs, enabling two sales from one product), a failing economy, as well as the September 11th attacks, the music industry is using file sharing and the downturn in global sales as excuses to cement further control over how music is distributed, accessed and consumed.

The music industry is reacting to the Internet and sales declines by implementing sweeping changes in order to further stabilize and guarantee its control over music. For example, in order to confront the Internet's potential ability to empower independent labels and artists, the music industry is creating a hyper-commercial media environment in which music is cross-promoted everywhere from Internet services to mobile phones to TV commercials. The conglomerated music industry is taking advantage of what its competitors do not have, immense horizontal and vertical capabilities to cross-promote products and establish name recognition. Here, conglomerate corporations can promote musical artists on their labels by placing them in the magazines, Internet sites, TV shows, movies, radio stations, and other outlets they own. They can also integrate artists more cheaply because conglomerate corporations often own all of the means of production and distribution. Indeed, name recognition and brand development will become increasingly important if the Internet places independent musicians on par with major labels. However, given the present media ownership and Internet architecture, this is extremely unlikely to occur.

The increasingly commercialized mode of industry operation means the manner in which music is consumed is changing from once being something mostly confined to the radio, home or car stereo, to being ubiquitous. Radio is no longer the dominant means of attaining new music anymore. Discovering new music now takes place through the Internet, video games, cell phones, television and movies. More and more music and musical artists are being promoted in commercials, the Internet, movies, video games, on cans of soda, as well as in other media and consumer products. Increasing the promotion of musical artists within and outside of conglomerate media holdings also has the benefit of increasing revenue from royalties, which stem from a complex system of rights associated with music ownership. Therefore, the music industry also makes money by placing its own music in media and advertisements. The result of this shameless self-promotion limits the range of culture and blurs the line between art and advertising. Indeed, the newly consolidated Big 4 music conglomerates have ownership and economic advantages over smaller independent labels, which enable them to dominate music markets with a few blockbuster artists.

To confront file sharing on the Internet, the music industry is viewing the transition into the digital realm as a new opportunity to control online distribution by securing copyright to new heights. In transitional times of uncertainty, one can correctly assume the music industry will make every effort to assure this new medium will work to its benefit. Indeed, it is working to assure additional revenue will be made in the future based on developing a favorable distribution architecture, as well as through new forms of copyright protection, even though their financial loses resulting from file sharing may not have been as damaging as their public relations departments would have wanted the public to believe (Alderman 2001; Christman 2001a; "Declining Music" 2003).

Indeed, the music industry is in the game for the long-haul and it is making sure the future is organized in such a way as to maximize its profits. The Big 4 have been developing technology to prevent CD copying and to limit file transferring and sharing even before global sales began declining in 2000. It is currently using legal intimidation, audio sabotage, policing tactics, as well as political lobbying to secure its interests. Finally, the music industry is in the process of colonizing every aspect of digital music sales, which will further consolidate the media industries and aid the major labels' goal of creating a world where making unauthorized copies of music will be illegal or impossible. In this new world, the music industry wants to regulate how people use and consume music, which ultimately questions the "fair use" clause in the U.S. Constitution. Fair use was intended to allow the public to make a copy of an artistic work for non-commercial purposes.

Besides working to prevent copying on and offline to increase sales, a number of other methods are being implemented to boost revenue. For example, an additional industry goal is to generate sales though new media requiring ever evolving expensive hardware. The new media and hardware also protect copyright, which has made hackers, as well as software and hardware manufactures struggle to find a means by which consumers can create copies of purchased music. In addition, another industry goal is to create new technology that features exclusive music, video or artist information in a number of dispersed for-pay services. Here, consumers have to pay subscription fees to various services in order to access exclusive music. If they want access to new music, they have to not only pay to subscribe to these Internet or wireless services, but they have to buy the music as well.

In addition, consumers also have to purchase video games and consoles if they want to hear new songs since in many cases they are not played on the radio or released in hardcopy format. Then, when the actual full-length CD is released a few months later, consumers may decide to purchase it as well enabling the music industry with at least "2 sales" of the same product. This "2 sales" phenomenon, where consumers end up purchasing the same music with additional hardware in several formats in order to listen to new releases is part of the music industry's overall business plan. Historically consumers already purchased music at least twice during the introduction of the compact disc. They first purchased albums and cassettes, then repurchased the same releases on a newer CD format requiring additional hardware. In fact, they may have purchased the same music on three formats if they bought 8-track tapes. Now, they may decide to do the same with newer CD and musical DVD formats, or through digital downloads or wireless subscription services. In fact, they may have to buy the same music in new formats in order to listen to it through different playback devices.

In essence, the music industry is creating a labyrinth of various locks and keys through diverse software and hardware, which open exclusive digital entertainment content. This well-connected maze also includes subscription-based doors that allow access to music, interviews, footage, and other material of interest to consumers. In many ways, this infrastructure is beginning to resemble a digital vending machine of sorts. In every digital nook and cranny opportunities to access or purchase items will be available for subscribers. As the music industry evolves, consumers will be likely to own fewer material formats, but will "rent" more and more music. Actual ownership may only entail the hardware that enables access to music or other digital cultural products such as film or video. Moreover, participating in this digital vending labyrinth will be an expensive "game." However, for those who can afford it, they will be rewarded by having the most information and new music from their favorite artists, which may increase their popularity, especially among younger consumers who look to music for inspiration and fashion.

QUESTIONS

This book asks a number of questions in its examination of recent changes in the music industry. The primary question asks how the music industry's business plan for digital distribution is affecting consumers? What kinds of technology are being implemented and how are they affecting the value of the music industry? How accurate is the music industry's claim that file sharing and CD copying are severely damaging the music business? These questions also raise additional concerns because the music industry is owned by conglomerate parent companies that make electronics, computer hardware, as well as own various media outlets. Therefore, how is industry conglomeration affecting the diversity of music, new services and audio equipment available to consumers? Finally, how are new technologies influencing consumer interactions and access to music, and what are the implications for consumers and culture?

IMPORTANCE

The music industry is important to study for a number of reasons. As the second largest media industry after film, the music industry enjoys an extremely large consumer base throughout the world (Dominick 2002). However, by 2007, the video game industry is expected to surpass the music industry in terms of value. Second, music is culture, culture is identity and identity often signifies the essence of a people. Music is also a platform enabling individuals or groups with the ability to critique social and cultural formations in society. Depending on the level of access and distribution, music can also enlighten the public by facilitating different voices and ideas through song. Given the increasing concentration of the industry, commercial music also serves as an example of how commerce and culture interact. Most importantly, the decisions being made by the music industry are radically altering the manner in which music is bought, delivered and consumed. Therefore it is imperative this transitional period be examined.

Moreover, the conglomerate-driven business plan for the music industry should also be seen as a pilot project for video game, television and movie development, which will also occur through online and wireless distribution. Access to exclusive or different versions of movies, television shows, radio shows and video games is likely to develop through a variety of subscription services and playback devices similar to the music industry. Because music industry development preceded movie distribution mostly due to bandwidth limitations, what is happening in the music industry should be seen as a precursor to what will happen with movies and television.

PART OF BROADER CORPORATE AND GOVERNMENTAL PRACTICES

Although there are more important and pressing matters facing the world today such as war, erosion of civil liberties and the rise of corporate power, the music industry does represent a broader trend of limiting access to goods and services based on financial status. Accessing education, information, prosperity and even disaster assistance is becoming increasingly difficult for people of lower and mid-level socio-economic status. For example, access to healthcare and quality care is becoming more difficult. Close to forty percent of the U.S. population lacks health insurance. Even though offer rates (the percentage of employees who work where insurance is offered) have slightly risen, eligibility rates and enrollment rates have decreased more dramatically since the mid-nineties through the early part of the twenty-first century (Stanton 2004). In addition, access to effective drugs and medication is becoming increasingly dependent on individual finance, which enables those who have more money to pay for better medication and healthcare. Access to college education is also becoming more difficult as tuition increases outweigh changes in inflation and growth in median family income (U.S. Department of Education 2004). In many areas across the United States, especially in New Orleans and St. Louis, the public school systems are failing, which means access to decent education requires money for private schools.

Access to information is also becoming more difficult (Lessig 1999; 2001; Shapiro 1999; Vaidhyanathan 2001). Databases and journals are becoming more expensive, which creates gaps between those who can afford information from those who cannot. Access to information can create opportunities and is needed in democratic societies for people to make informed decisions. Even accessing the so-called American dream of social mobility through hard work in a promising job is also becoming more difficult (Vogel 2006).

Finally, emergency care and disaster assistance also appear to favor those with financial resources. Access to resources needed for survival, as in the case of the 2005 levee breach in New Orleans, meant that many who could not afford care or assistance on their own where left to die, and die they did. Over one thousand people were killed not only by the government's failure to protect its own citizens by creating levees that work, but also by the government's later failure and inability to evacuate victims and provide assistance. In fact, even for Americans abroad, survival may increasingly depend on quick access to money during emergencies. For example, during the one month Israeli invasion of Lebanon, the U.S. government tried to charge U.S. citizens for the cost of their own evacuation (Klein 2006). Again, although not as important as these services, the music industry is following the broader trend of limiting access to goods and services based on economic status.

DESCRIPTION OF REMAINING CHAPTERS

The following chapter will describe the methods used in this investigation, as well as introduce theory on new technology and social change. Two main perspectives—utopian and dystopian—dominate the theoretical playing field. Utopians tend to view technology and its effects on society in generally positive terms, while dystopians are more critical noting technology has yet to create a more equitable and just world. Both perspectives are analyzed while discussing their ramifications for political change, social interaction, industry consolidation, political power, as well as control over information and culture. These perspectives are used to guide this book with a general contextualization and framework for some of the changes occurring within the music industry. Indeed, new technologies appear to be enabling macro shifts within various modes of operation for the music industry.

Chapter 3 looks at the Big 4 record companies that manufacture most of the world's music. Ownership is important to examine because owners make decisions that influence not only the music people hear, but also where and how they listen to it. Having an understanding of media ownership also contextualizes the remaining chapters because they focus on different consequences of conglomeration for consumers and culture. Because conglomerates have holdings in various media, Internet, electronics, and technology companies, they can easily cross-promote their own content, as well as save money on production costs. The music industry's market share, consolidation, recent revenue, and ownership patterns are also examined as they affect cultural diversity. Finally, established modes of production resulting from ownership patterns are investigated. The music industry is trimming artist rosters, promoting fewer artists, relying on fewer production companies, as well as using new software to determine hit songs. These trends also affect retail stores through their decision to cut back on CD selections. As a result of these recent developments, this chapter argues mainstream music is becoming less diverse due to industry concentration and pressure to increase revenue.

Chapter 4 focuses on how the music industry is dramatically increasing the commercialization of musical artists at a time when artist rosters are shrinking. It also examines how this increase is affecting musicians and culture. It first discusses the modes of promotion popularly utilized within the industry including promotion outside of, within and across media and products, co-branding between companies and circular marketing tactics such as "price points and "cleans" that attempt to measure the degree of media exposure for a given product and subsequently create hype. It then explores how cross-promotion not only benefits companies by reducing advertising costs, but also by producing steady and reliable revenue in the form of royalties garnered from publishing rights held by music companies. In this scenario, more exposure yields additional profits making cross-promotion a handsome prospect, especially when corporations have the ability to cross-promote within their own conglomerate holdings. Finally hyper-commercialism may subjugate musicians to the marketing demands of the handful of companies that determine which artists are granted viable exposure. In short, hyper-commercialism sparked by conglomerate business warps music culture into an advertising blitz for corporations, while muddling the line between culture and commerce.

Chapter 5 also examines aspects of conglomeration. It investigates the connections between the Big 4 and various electronics and computer manufacturers by looking at new hardware such as CD burners, MP3 players and video game consoles. Because Big 4 parent companies such as Vivendi/Universal, Electric & Musical Industries (EMI) and Sony also manufacture computer and electronics equipment, the music industry ironically makes money from what it argues is hurting sales. It stands to gain from CD burning and downloading through the sales of various electronics devices and software programs. Finally, it investigates new media the music industry is hoping will replace standard CDs in hopes of gaining additional sales. It argues the industry sparks multiple sales from one product by combining new hardware and communication services with exclusive music, as well as with the invention of new media forms. By dividing music into various products and services, the industry hopes to conquer wallets and purses through the sales of new technologies and services.

Chapter 6 traces the value of the Big 4 from 1999 to 2005, a period the music industry argues incurred incredible financial loses due to file sharing through services such as Napster and Kazaa. Because each music division exists within a conglomerate that makes a number of different products and services linked to their music divisions, accurate estimates of exact value are quite difficult. While Chapters 4 and 5 examined the revenue conglomerates earn through cross-promotion and profits from electronic hardware such as video game consoles, DVD, and MP3 players, as well as CD burning and blank discs, this chapter focuses on additional production-oriented mechanisms that influence the economic wellbeing of the music industry. It examines how artist rosters, the elimination of CD singles, and the economy affect industry value. It also describes how new media sales, increases in artist, marketing and production costs, employee lay-offs, the end of the CD-replacement cycle, changing demographics,

and used CD sales influence profits for the Big 4. As a result, this chapter argues the net result of sales decreases during 2000–2003 did not mean the music industry was going bankrupt or "out of business."

While chapter 6 introduced and examined various influences that affect the value of the music industry, chapter 7 focuses on the music industry's response to challenges in copyright infringement, which it claims to be driving recent sales losses. It begins by examining the notion of "fair use" and how it is related to the debate on file sharing and CD copying. The second part describes the music industry's success in influencing the legal system through its political lobby group, which has been able to write laws, as well as manipulate various political platforms in its favor. The third section describes how laws have enabled the creation of different forms of digital rights management technologies, as well as how they work. Because the public's reception to these new laws and technologies has not been warm, the music industry has transformed itself into a pseudo policing organization in its pursuit of counter-fitters and file-traders. Finally, although these industry pursuits would assume large numbers of people are downloading music and that sales are down, surveys from the Pew Center, Ipos Reid and the NPD Group suggest the opposite. Therefore, because the industry started developing digital rights management technology at a time when music sales were at an all time high, this chapter argues the music industry is using its wealth and political influence to manipulate the legal system in its favor, while using fear of arrest as a means of forcing people into subscribing to "legitimate," or Big 4 supported music services. The result of these industry tactics threatens two things: the constitutionally protected notion of "fair use" and the public's ability to operate free from government and private interests in the online world.

Chapter 8 continues examining the digital realm by focusing on the music industry's transition into online distribution. It looks at digital music services and their impact on consumers and retail while examining the connections the Big 4 are making with Internet service providers (ISPs), Web sites that offer music downloads for sale, as well as with hardware and software manufacturing companies. The transition is fueling further industry consolidation and concentration. This chapter also examines the tiered system of online music subscription services and how ownership affects public access to online digital music. Because each service offers different labels and exclusive content, consumers need to subscribe to several services in order to fully access a variety of tunes. Finally, the impact of the Big 4's entry into online sales on traditional retail stores and their reaction to this transition are also examined. There is a race between retailers, distributors, and record companies for online music markets. This chapter argues the Big 4's transition into digital music sales will give the music industry more control over online music, more profits when compared with hardcopy formats, as well as more revenue as it begins to take away profits once associated with traditional retail. Because music is becoming divided throughout several subscription-based services, the music industry is creating a divide between wealthy consumers who will have money to pay for these over-priced services and downloads from those who cannot afford to have full access.

Chapter 9 parallels chapter 8's argument, but the medium changes from the Internet to wireless. It notes the trends in the music and wireless distribution market are extensions of the music industry's pre-wireless business plan. There is a continuation of the division of music by label, timing and exclusive content, as well as a continuation of subscription fees. In addition, this new platform is characterized by oligopolistic pricing and exhibits a continuation of the lock and key strategy. This strategy continues forcing consumers into purchasing different media, hardware, and services in order to access music. Finally, chapter 10 wraps up the previous chapters, reiterates the researcher's main argument, and offers suggestions for change.

CHAPTER 2

THEORETICAL PERSPECTIVES ON TECHNOLOGY AND METHODOLOGY

UTOPIAN AND DYSTOPIAN PERSPECTIVES ON TECHNOLOGY

Understanding broader theory on new technology helps contextualize issues permeating within the music industry in at least two ways. First, familiarization with theory on a macro level helps contextualize and connect broader trends with specific examples within the music industry. Second, the music industry is using new forms of technology to change the manner in which music is accessed and consumed.

New communication technology is often described through utopian and dystopian terms (Wellman 1997; Fischer and Wright 2001). While utopians see technology and its effects on society in overwhelmingly positive terms, dystopians are more critical. Although dystopians are not technology cheerleaders, they are not completely against it either, as such a dichotomy may suggest. Most critics, although referred to as dystopians, lie somewhere in between utopians and so-called dystopians. Although their critiques of new technologies do not infer that a revolution is going on, they would certainly like to see one. Dystopians rarely see any macro social changes leading to the conclusion that the world is becoming a more equitable and just place as a result of new technology. In fact, they see a trend toward too much private control over information with negative social ramifications for Internet usage, as well as unenthusiastic political implications and damage to the public sphere.

UTOPIAN PERSPECTIVES

Several authors focusing on new technology suggest the Internet may create better communities while enabling new forms of social liberation. Authors such as Jones (1998), Baym (1998), Rheingold (1993) and Levy (1997) claim the Internet not only cultivates new identities and forms of communities, but that these communities may be qualitatively better than traditional offline communities. In fact, these scholars suggest "cyber-communities" will be just as important to society as normal "communities." Danet (1998) and Clark (1998) agree, noting the Internet can liberate people from oppressive social norms.

Pavlik (1998) and Goldstein (1994) also see positive political changes resulting from the Internet. They suggest the Internet will allow greater freedom, more choices, as well as provide easier access to information. Although all media content will come through highly centralized media organizations (Goldstein 1994), Pavlik and Goldstein see little problem with this. This counters general theory on media and democracy, which suggests the media are far from democratic when consolidated and left to the private sector (Bagdikian 1993; Herman and McChesney 1997; Keane 1991; Lee and Solomon 1990; Mazzocco 1994; McChesney 1997, 2000a; Wasko 1993).

Nonetheless, other utopian scholars profess new technology holds promise to break up existing industry structures while creating a more democratic public sphere. According to the Association for Progressive Communications (1997), the Internet is a new and powerful force that will democratize communications. It may even give voice to the powerless (Fisher 1998) while resurrecting the public sphere with unmediated discourse (Coleman 1999). It may even revive democratic processes (Poster 1997) and offer a new kind of public sphere or replace the old sphere damaged by fragmentation and commodification (Tsagarousianou 1998).

Howard Rheingold (1993) also suggests the Internet has extreme potential as a democratizing force, while Shapiro (1999) argues the Internet is allowing individuals to take power away from government, mass media and corporate institutions. Internet-connected citizens are only beginning to take control over resources, information and experience. In effect, the Internet will place the means of production over informational resources into the hands of citizens, which according to Shapiro, is truly egalitarian.

Similar to Shapiro, John Perry Barlow also suggests the Internet holds potential to undermine corporate and commercial control of the media. He noted big media firms are merely "rearranging deck chairs on the Titanic" (McChesney 2000b). The logic here holds that if everything is in the process of being digital, and if anyone can produce a Website at a minimal cost, then it is just a matter of time before the media giants find themselves swamped by competitors (McChesney 2000b).

Utopian arguments have a number of limitations. In many ways, utopians can be described as future forecasters basing their arguments on speculation and potential, rather than on a broad number of actual occurrences. Most utopians are also technological determinists, who rarely connect the trajectory of technology with political decisions made by humans. Seldom will the role of human agency be cited in these perspectives. Finally, while almost every new technology can have benefits, most have limitations as well. It is fairly obvious utopians are excited about the technology they use and discuss. As a result, they tend to speak highly about them. It is no wonder so-called "dystopians" are more reactionary to utopian claims when only potential benefits are discussed by utopians. Nonetheless, value can be found in utopian abilities to think positively about the potential social ramifications that technology *could* bring for humanity.

DYSTOPIAN PERSPECTIVES

Dystopians paint a much darker picture of the Internet's potential to democratize institutions. Tambini (1999) suggests the claims of most civic networkers are naive. The idea that new media will erode existing political hierarchies and replace them with a new egalitarian and democratic fabric of civil society is misleading. The degree to which new forms of technology enable democratic participation will depend on how the media are regulated, who has access and how choices will be made (Tambini 1999). Indeed, technological utopianism is based not only on the belief in the magic of technology over human agency, but also that capitalism is a fair, rational and democratic mechanism, which is a myth (McChesney 2000b).

Scholars such as Lessig (1999; 2001), Shapiro (1999), and Vaidhyanathan (2001) also suggest people will be less free to access information and other cultural goods in the future. This is partially due to copyright control, which has been another means of maintaining corporate control and power after industry downturns (Freedman 2003). The creation of the industry-supported Digital Copyright Millennium Act (DCMA) made it illegal to circumvent anti-piracy technologies, which essentially left copyright in the hands of corporations (Vaidhyanathan 2004; Lessig 2005). While copyright eventually expires and allows for fair use, the DCMA allows content owners to dictate all content use, regardless of copyright law, as long as the content has been encoded. Many scholars believe that copyright legislation has shifted to protect investment rather than creativity (Viera 2003; Lessig 2005; Bates 2004; Vaidhyanathan 2004). Lessig (2005) also argues that because of hyperactive copyright and extreme conglomeration, a small minority now has the legal right to control culture. Under current circumstances corporations censor culture and the state simply supports it (Vaidhyanathan 2004). Corporations have been able use legislation and technology to retrench and enforce the power structure. According to McCourt and Burkart (2003), "while new technologies initially appear to challenge and undermine the control of the established systems, they can ultimately benefit the status quo" (9). If these scholars turn out to be correct, people will have limited access to ideas and perspectives, which can harm individual reflection and deliberation as a result of content unavailability.

Besides providing control over information to the government and private sector, the Internet may create negative social effects for heavy users. People may close their horizons by narrowing their exposure to different ideas and perspectives, which can limit opportunities, free speech, privacy, as well as personal experiences. Kolko and Reid (1998) and Sunstein (2001) note people may be becoming fragmented and isolated resulting from new communication technologies. Wilhelm (2000) also suggests the Internet will make it easier for people to remove themselves from public life, which may result in decreased civic engagement.

Besides social implications of technological changes, there are also political implications resulting from technological changes. Both implications are connected given that restricted access to information can also be political. Similar to Lessig (2001) and Shapiro (1999), scholars such as McChesney (2000b), Herman and McChesney (1997) and Schiller (1999) all note the current trajectory of the Internet will benefit private interests more that the public interest, which may have negative effects concerning political liberties and public communication. Political liberties may be jeopardized due to surveillance and lack of access to information, while public communication through the Internet will go through commercial services requiring fees, which may shut out certain segments of the population.

NEW TECHNOLOGY AND THE MUSIC INDUSTRY

While new technology theorists are often labeled utopian or dystopian, much of the debate over how new technology will affect music and culture centers on similar issues. The first issue is the Internet's potential to break up the highly concentrated music industry. Here the Internet is viewed as having potential to break up existing industry structures because no one will need a major label to promote them anymore. Some scholars and famous musicians see the Internet as having this potential to break up and democratize the music industry. According to Columbia Law School Professor Eben Moglen, the major labels will "be competed out of business by anarchism, which works better. The only hope for those dead businesses is if they realize they are dead and begin to reinvent themselves" (Carlozo 2001). Famous rock musician Elton John noted on the Today show in March of 2000 that publishers are "thieves" and "blatant, out-and-out crooks" and that the major labels are now "laughing all the way to the bank." However, John also suggested "they won't be laughing very soon, because when the music on the Internet comes in, the record companies will all be crying" (Mann 2000). In addition, Chuck D of Public Enemy, a well-known hip-hop artist who supports and encourages digital exchange of music over the Internet, suggested "the execs, lawyers and accountants . . . are now running scared from the technology that evens out the creative field and makes artists harder to pimp" (Greenfeld 1999).

Indeed, new technology may have the ability to empower independent artists. Musicians can now bypass larger labels through marketing music on their own Websites, as well as through peer-to-peer file sharing. These capabilities resonate not only with more general macro new technology scholars such as Rheingold (1993) and Shapiro (1999), but also with more recent work on the music industry. However, these perspectives largely ignore other important areas of cultural influence such as distribution, decreasing concert promoters for venues and radio airplay.

Nonetheless, other scholars suggest the Internet will not dramatically change the way in which the media and music industry operate. Dolfsma (2000) suggests the Internet will not dramatically change the composition of the music industry. He notes technological developments create economic environments for traditional players in the music industry that are highly uncertain. Information technology and the Internet allow musicians to offer their music directly to their "customers," which creates opportunities for new intermediaries to enter the market and offer a mix of new and old services. These developments, according to Dolfsma, pose a threat to existing music industry intermediaries such as music publishers, record companies and retail outlets. However, he suggests these intermediaries or "gatekeepers" will continue to exist and that the Internet will not change the industry as much as others predict.

However, Mann (2000) suggests the music industry may gain additional control as a result of the Internet and changes in digital copyright law. Indeed, the music industry's push for regulation over the distribution of culture is inconsistent with the conception of the commons that lies at the root of democracy. According to legal scholar Lawrence Lessig, "people hear the cries of the industry about piracy, which are real and justifiable . . . but they don't realize that simply giving the industry what it wants will have an impact on the entire public sphere" (Mann 2000). Here, the suggestion is that when a few companies control the rights to distribution of a cultural product, grass-roots cultural expression may become impeded.

To conclude, one can note that definitions of identity and perspective concerning the music industry's relationship with the Internet differ depending on the author's technological outlook. As a result, utopian and dystopian perspectives carry different ramifications concerning the social and political effects that new technologies may have on society. Because changes resulting from new technological developments are only now beginning to take hold, critical work in the area of new technology and music appears to be an under-studied area in need of more attention.

METHODOLOGY

This section describes the methods used to gather data for this book. It first describes the strengths of a qualitative research approach while discussing this study's primary and secondary sources. It continues to explain why a political economy approach was the most useful for this book. Natural inquiry was also used because the author has been involved in the music industry for over fifteen years as an independent musician, music producer, small record label co-owner, consumer, and radio dj. In many ways, some of the topics included in this analysis are results of real life experiences and conversations with various people affiliated with the music business.

Because this is a contemporary history, primary sources are defined as music industry practices conveyed through trade journals. Practices are the "raw material" being analyzed. Therefore, primary sources consisted of corporate press releases and industry articles in online and offline trade journals such as Billboard, Music Industry News Network (Mi2N), Music & Copyright, Sound and Vision, Wired Magazine, and others gathered from January 1999 through early 2006. In total, hundreds of issues from Billboard Magazine, Music & Copyright, and other articles from various Mi2N issues were used to collect information and trends concerning the music industry.

Additional sources consisted of articles in business and technology sections of mainstream news publications such as CNN, the New York Times, Los Angeles Times, MSNBC, as well as other business publications. Although these articles often consist of arguments based on music industry press releases, they are useful because they provide industry claims that can be analyzed. These articles may also focus on music industry trends from an investor perspective, which can be helpful by providing supplemental sales and ownership information. Corporate databases such as Hoovers Company Database and Informamedia.com were also investigated because they provide useful economic and ownership information. Ironically, some databases required access fees registering in the thousands of dollars. For example, Music & Copyright charges $1,590 per year, while Billboard charges up to $849 per year depending on what kind of access one wants. Without access to some of these sources, the completion of this book would have been impossible. Thanks to several personal connections, I was able to access some of these databases for free. Finally, scholarly work on the music industry, new technology, copyright law, advertising, and political economy was also used to inform this investigation.

POLITICAL ECONOMY

A political and economic approach is used in this investigation. Instead of focusing on cultural texts, lyrics, music videos, gender relations, or race to find social meanings, which many other cultural studies scholars focus on, political economists focus on ownership, economics, and power relations, as well as cultural effects of these agents in their analyses. Political economists examining popular media acknowledge the fact that producers of mass media are industrial institutions essentially driven by the pursuit of profit maximization in a capitalist economy (Shuker 2001). Bourdieu (1993) suggests that cultural practices, cultural fields, power relations, trajectories, and works of individual agents must be taken into consideration in order to fully understand cultural works. In addition, the role of culture in the reproduction of social structures, power relations, inequities, as well as their roles in the classification systems of culture are also important to examine. This author takes Bourdieu's suggestions into consideration and focuses on how power dynamics are changing in the music industry as a result of new technologies. Indeed, computers and the Internet are changing nearly every aspect of the music industry from production to consumption (Alderman 2001).

In this case a political and economic approach is beneficial given its focus on power relations because musical artists, music corporations and consumers are struggling over the development of the Internet and its relationship to music. According to Mosco (1996), a political economy perspective focuses on social relations, particularly power relations that mutually constitute the production, distribution and consumption of resources. McChesney (2000a) also notes the scholarly study of political economy of mass communication examines how media and media content influence existing class and social relations. It also examines how ownership, support mechanisms such as advertising and government policies influence media behavior and content. McQuail (1994) expands on these ideas noting a political economy approach to media studies often focuses on the relationship between media ownership and the ideological content of media. Indeed, a number of scholars such as McChesney (2000a), Bagdikian (1992) and Herman and Chomsky (1988) have noted a link between media ownership, control and media content, which ultimately questions basic tenets of democratic communication.

If done well, a political and economic analysis guides research and provides suggestions for change based on a normative model grounded in egalitarian access to, and control over, informational and cultural resources. Industries that produce and transmit culture should reflect grass-roots creations from a wide array of peoples, ideas, and cultures. In addition, cultural productions should be easily accessible to the public through reasonable prices and services, which should result from public deliberation.

As a subset of postpositivist critical qualitative research, political economy may retain one of the most beneficial normative models for researchers concerned with democracy and social justice. Indeed, the political economy of communication has a strong "normative critique for the ways in which state policies and the methods by which media are owned, managed and subsidized affect the capacity of the media to serve this 'democratic function'" (McChesney 1998). It also embraces a commitment toward equality and democracy in society as well as in cultural and political institutions (Banks 1996). Ultimately, the purpose of a political economic critique is to assist in the process of social change, both in terms of "specific media policies within the context of a capitalist political economy and in terms of assisting broader social change toward a post capitalist and more democratic society. Unlike most cultural studies and quantitative studies, a political economy approach does not presuppose capitalist society as a given and does not discount structural factors in explaining media behavior" (McChesney 1998). For this reason, political economy, as a subset of critical theory, has an activist orientation interested in social change (Denzin and Lincoln 1998).

Nonetheless, political economy is often critiqued by some cultural studies scholars as being economically deterministic or reductionistic. Critics indicate that culture and ideology can operate outside of the economic realm. Some political economists such as Murdock and Golding (1979) agree that the economic base does not always dictate cultural form or content, while other political economists such as Garnham (1981) suggest the economic base does have the greatest influence on media content. With whatever lenses one examines culture, one can suggest there are different levels of commercialism within culture. As a result, it is difficult to make blanket statements concerning the degree to which economic factors dominate. Culture outside the market system may not be commercially driven, while most cultural productions within the culture industry are no doubt profit-driven.

CHAPTER 3

DESCRIPTION OF THE MUSIC INDUSTRY

While the previous chapter examined general theory on new technology and how it may be impacting the music industry, this chapter describes the companies that produce, own and control the technology that enables most of world's music to exist. Ownership is important to examine because owners ultimately make decisions that influence not only the music people hear, but also where and how they listen to it. Having an understanding of media ownership will also contextualize the remaining chapters because they focus on different consequences of conglomerate ownership for consumers and culture. Therefore, this chapter describes the major record labels as part of larger conglomerates, which are companies that own different media, Internet, electronics and technology companies. Because they own a number of different holdings, conglomerates are able to easily cross-promote their own content, as well as save money on production costs. The music industry's market share, consolidation, recent revenue, and ownership patterns are also examined because they ultimately affect the range of culture the public is exposed to. Finally, the established modes of production resulting from ownership patterns are also investigated. The music industry is trimming artist rosters, promoting fewer artists, relying on fewer production companies, as well as using new software to determine hit songs. These trends are also affecting retail stores through their decision to cut back on CD selections. As a result of these recent developments, this chapter argues pop music is becoming increasingly less diverse due to industry concentration and pressure to increase revenue.

Until recently the global music industry consisted of five transnational corporations that controlled roughly eighty percent of the recording, production and distribution of the world's music (Banks 1996; Burnett 1996; Croteau and Hoynes, 2000; Kelley 2002). In 2004 the Federal Trade Commission (FTC) and European Commission (EC) approved the merger of two of the former five corporations (Buck and Burt 2004; Ahrens 2004). As a result, four major conglomerates referred to as the "Big 4" now control the majority of the global music market.

Of all the mass media, the music industry employs the fewest workers. Not counting performers, there are only fifteen to eighteen thousand employees even though the music industry is the second largest media industry after the film industry (Dominick 2002). Nonetheless, this will soon change as the video gaming industry is expected to surpass the music industry and become the second largest media industry. The vast majority of music provided to retail stores comes from the following four companies: Sony-Bertlesmann Music Group (Sony-BMG), Time Warner's Warner Music Group (WMG), Vivendi/Universal's Universal Music Group (UMG), and Electric & Musical Industries (EMI).

Time Warner sold its music unit for $2.6 billion in 2003 in order to recover from its debt-ridden merger with AOL. It sold its music division to Seagram heir Edgar Bronfman Jr. and the investment firm Thomas H. Lee (Kirkpatrick 2003b). Nonetheless, Time Warner is still interested in buying back some of the unit in the future. WMG ownership consists of Thomas H. Lee Partners (49.8 percent), Bronfman's Lexa Partners (12.5 percent), Bain Capital (21.3 percent), Providence Equity Partners (11 percent), Edgar Bronfman Jr (2.9 percent), and Lyor Cohen (2.1 percent) (Christman 2004c). Warner Music Group and EMI are next in line for an expected potential merger. If they merge, there will be three companies that manufacture the majority of the world's music. On an interesting note, the industry has used piracy as an excuse for these mega mergers, conglomeration, cutbacks, and layoffs (McCourt and Burkart 2003).

Each Big 4 company is also part of a larger conglomerate corporation owning several other media outlets useful for vertical or horizontal integration. Here, production, distribution, and marketing divisions of a company are integrated throughout various media holdings to further reduce the costs of production and increase income. As one can see in chart 1, all of the Big 4 parent companies own holdings in other areas associated with media, entertainment and electronics. For example, Sony-BMG owns a number of holdings in publishing, broadcasting, book & music clubs, online retail channels, consumer electronics, movies, TV programming, DVDs, semiconductors, game consoles, and PCs.

Vivendi/Universal also has ownership of TV, games, wireless, cable, movies, theme parks, and telecom, while EMI has holdings in CDs, videos, and publishing. Seagram combined with Vivendi and Canal+ Television in 2000, which created Vivendi Universal. Seagram also owns the Universal Studios film company. In 2004, Vivendi Universal Entertainment also merged with NBC to form NBC Universal.

Because the Big 4 are owned by conglomerates, the music industry can easily cross-promote its own content, as well as earn revenue from sales of electronic products. The conglomeration of the music industry can also affect culture and access to music, which are the foci of Chapters 4 and 5.

MUSIC INDUSTRY CONGLOMERATE INTERESTS 2005

Vivendi-Universal	TV, games, wireless, cable, movies, theme parks, telecom
Sony BMG	Publishing, broadcasting, book & music clubs, online retail channels, consumer electronics, movies, TV programming, DVDs, semicondu game consoles, PCs, etc...
EMI	CD, videos, publishing
Time Warner	ISPs, browsers, film, TV, publishing, cable, professional sports, interactive services

Chart 1; Source: Hoovers.com 2005; Dominick 2002.

In terms of market share, chart 2 shows that Vivendi/Universal's UMG is the world's largest music company encompassing 26 percent of the global market. The Sony-BMG merger created the second largest music conglomerate holding with a market of share of 22 percent. EMI comes in third place with a share of 13 percent, and Warner Music Group, the smallest of the Big 4, holds on to 11 percent of the market. Finally, the hundreds of thousands of other music labels around the world account for the remaining 28 percent.

GLOBAL MARKET SHARE 2004

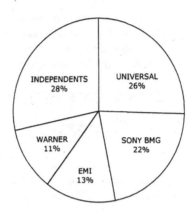

Chart 2; Source: IFPI, August 2, 2005.

Almost all of the Big 4 have ever changing joint ventures with each other. For example, Warner Music has entered into a licensing agreement with EMI Music to manufacture, market, and distribute Warner's catalogue in India, effectively turning the Big 4 into the Big 3 in that market ("Warner is Music" 2005.) UMG has a joint venture with Sony selling music online through a company called PressPlay. In mid 2003, Roxio was to acquire PressPlay and relaunch it under the Napster name (Mathews 2003), and by 2004 Sony merged with BMG. Columbia House record club was also a joint venture between Sony Music Entertainment and AOL/Time Warner ("Sony Music Entertainment" 2003) until 2005, when BMG Direct, parent of BMG Music Service acquired Columbia House for roughly $400 million. This merger combined the two largest direct-to-consumer companies of music in the United States. They have an annual revenue of $1.5 billion with sixteen million members in North America, although most of Columbia House's sales now come from DVD sales (Garrity 2005c).

All of the Big 4-related music publishing divisions also work together in joint ventures and often decide prices together. Sony BMG Music Entertainment, BMG Publishing, EMI Music Publishing, Warner/Chappell Music, Universal Music Group, and EMI Music Publishing have made deals with each other concerning master ringtones, DualDiscs, videos, and digital rights (Garrity 2005e). Sony BMG and EMI Publishing also defined rates for master ringtones, ringbacks, and dualdisc and video rates, while part of EMI's musical copyrights come from its acquisition of CBS Songs, the earlier publishing business of CBS records, which Sony Music Label Group U.S. now owns. So EMI and Sony also have in many ways a joint venture together (Garrity 2005f). Sony owns the music and EMI owns the copyrights good for royalties. Finally, UMG and WMG formed a joint venture called Royalty Services, which is in charge of royalty accounting for both companies (Garrity 2004e). TimeWarner, EMI, and Sony joined with Comcast and Cox to co-own Music Choice, a cable service that provides audio and will eventually provide music videos (Hansell 2004d). In addition nearly all of the Big 4 have further joint ventures in distribution, online retail, Internet sites, or through investment in smaller labels.

Given the dominance of so few companies, the music industry is an oligopoly. It is a market controlled by an extremely small number of companies, which enables them to set prices and create "barriers to entry" against competition by lowering prices or by using their cross-promotional power to advertise their products over those of potential competitors. The Big 4 are also transnational corporations "based" in several different countries. Sony-BMG's headquarters are located in New York (though Sony is based in Japan and Bertelsmann is headquartered in Germany), Time Warner is from the U.S., EMI Distribution is from the U.K., while Vivendi/Universal is from France.

Roughly seventy percent of these companies' revenues come from outside the United States given that the Big 4 operate in countries all over the world. For example, UMG has operations in 71 countries, Sony Music (pre-merger) in 60 countries, Warner Music in 70 countries, and EMI in over 50 countries. These companies are often described as gatekeepers that allow certain kinds of music to be promoted and determine which types will be rejected. They also make decisions based on financial gain rather than for cultural or educational purposes (Banks 1996; Burnett 1996; Campbell 2000).

A BRIEF HISTORY OF MUSIC CONSOLIDATION

The concentration of the music industry is not a product of the modern era (Peterson and Berger 1975). During the early part of the twentieth century, three firms dominated the phonograph industry. The Edison Phonograph Company, the Victor Talking Machine Company and the Columbia Graphophone Company (later to be known as Columbia) held a tight oligopoly until the Depression, where RCA and Decca Records took over the other labels accept for Columbia. Capital Records came along in the 1940s to create a fourth company (Roberts 2002). The late 1950s saw an increase in independent labels when radio stations began to target specialized markets. Rhythm & blues and rock & roll music helped these labels compete with the majors to such an extent that by the mid-to-late 1950s, there were at times close to twenty-nine different record companies being represented on the Top Ten charts. From roughly 1959–1963 a period of secondary consolidation occurred with eight firms acquiring half of the market share, even though there were forty labels competing (Peterson and Berger 1975). Beatlemania and the California sound of the 1960s spurred more growth in firms until the 1970s, where the industry consolidated with Columbia,

Warner Brothers, Capitol, and Motown dominating market shares. Independents were increasingly being pushed out of the industry by the expensive costs associated with breaking new bands. They were competing with major label advertising budgets often ranging in the hundreds of thousands of dollars. The 1980s saw further consolidation with major labels incorporating, or "co-opting" punk music, while MCA purchased Motown. In addition, Island Records was also sold to Polygram and rap became commercialized as well (Shuker 2001). By the 1990s, the music industry had been thoroughly gobbled up by international transnationals marking another high point of consolidation by becoming more integrated within both vertical and horizontal outlets (Hull 2000).

Although already highly concentrated, more consolidation for the music industry is expected for the future. According to entertainment magazine Billboard, "Consolidation among the major record labels is not only inevitable but imminent" (Benz, Christman, and Garrity, 2003). Mergers are more likely to occur when "corporate friendly" commissioners are appointed to various regulatory commissions. The Bush Jr. administration was just the kind of political ally needed to create an environment conducive of further consolidation. Sony Music and BMG successfully merged in 2004 under their watch with EC and FTC approval, which reduced the industry to the "Big 4." A year earlier, AOL/Time Warner's Warner Music Group, Bertelsmann's BMG and EMI were also in discussions to combine their music divisions (Holloway 2003b; Kirkpatrick 2003a). Because EMI owns the fewest platforms to publicize and distribute its music, it is the worst off when compared to AOL/Time Warner, which owns numerous media outlets to promote its music. The major labels were (and are) interested in merging due to a mutual concern with cost-cutting and restructuring. As with Sony BMG, the aim was to combine and form an economy of scale compatible with UMG which owns the largest market share. Indeed, Sony Music and Bertelsmann's BMG merger was expected to save an estimated $300-360 million annually for the newly merged company ("Music Slump" 2004; "Sony Music-BMG Merger Sails," 2004). If an EMI-Warner merger is permitted by the U.S government, these acquisitions would further consolidate and blur a market already characterized by extreme concentration. A short-lived Big 4 could become the Big 3, which would mean that three companies would manufacture roughly eighty percent of all music sold around the world. This in itself is astonishing and the ramifications in terms of creating a more diverse culture are devastating.

PARENT COMPANIES AND ECONOMICS OF EMPIRE

The parent companies that own the Big 4 music divisions are huge media empires spreading into nearly every media form imaginable. Given their size, they generate enormous profits larger than the economies of several nations around the world.

Parent companies generate huge profits with their vast media empires. Vivendi Universal's revenue for 2002 was $67,890,125,000, while its net worth was $16,345,000,000. Sony's revenue registered at $62,437,268,000, while its net worth was $47,912,957,000. AOL/Time Warner came in at $40,961,000,000 for revenue, while its net worth was $52,817,000,000. Bertelsmann is worth $7,991,111,040 with revenues of $18,896,335,920 for 2002. Finally, EMI is at the bottom of the barrel with a reported revenue of $3,785,300,000 and a net worth of $1,116,700,000 (Lexis-Nexis Database).

By 2005 some of these numbers have decreased, but remain impressive:

REVENUE AND NET WORTH: PARENT COMPANY

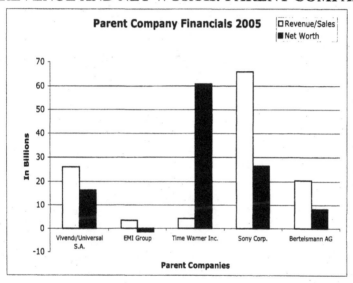

Graph A; Source: Corporate Affiliations via Lexis-Nexis, Nov. 2005.

Even though they generate large sums of money, music divisions within parent companies are not priorities. While parent companies are growing larger through mergers, the music divisions are becoming less important because they bring in a smaller percentage of overall sales. For example, in the quarter ending in December of 2001, Sony's music division only accounted for 9.1 percent of the parent companies total revenue. WMG's revenue made up only 10.3 percent of AOL Time Warner's total sales. Its earnings only accounted for 4.2 percent of the company total. UMG, with its largest market share of all the music companies, still only had a revenue of roughly 34 percent of Vivendi Universal's total (Benz 2002). Nonetheless, their income has increased dramatically over the past two decades.

MUSIC INDUSTRY REVENUES (1973–2003)

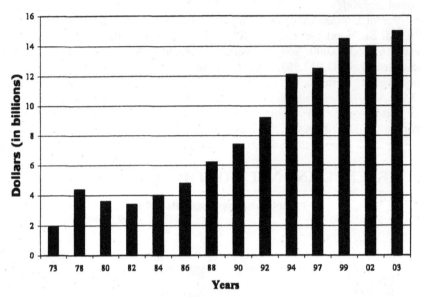

Graph B; Source: Dominick 2002, 217; Holson 2003a, Kelley 2002.

Graph B clearly shows the music industry dramatically increased its revenues from 1980 to 2003. In fact, they increased five-fold. Unfortunately music sales had been falling during the seventies until roughly 1983, when the invention of the compact disc resurrected sales turning the industry into a cash cow for the following twenty years. Domestic sales of CDs skyrocketed from 800,000 copies in 1983 to 288 million by 1990 and continued to increase by hundreds of millions throughout the 1990s ("Why Experts" 2003). Although the industry's profits stagnated again during the mid-nineties, they increased by 20 percent from 1997–1999 because of an average price increase of $3.00 per compact disc. By 2000, the industry entered an agreement with the FTC to stop this pricing practice after an investigation into anti-trust practices (Dominick 2002). During the two years leading up to this agreement, file sharing services such as Napster also began to appear, challenging industry notions of distribution, copyright, ownership, and consumption. Slumping music sales paralleled this introduction, which led, and continues to lead the music industry to blame these services for the decrease. However, a number of factors suggest that services such as Napster had a minimal economic impact on industry sales (please see chapter 6 for a break down of additional influences). As one can see, revenues for the music industry have clearly increased during the past twenty to twenty-five years.

On an international basis, worldwide music sales create revenues of $40 billion per year (Vogel 2001). In terms of a reference point, the music industry is worth more than the combined Gross Domestic Product (GDP) of the following ten counties: Equatorial Guinea, Djibouti, Comoros, Chad, Eritrea, Cape Verde, Burundi, Burkina Faso, Benin, and Angola (US International Trade Commission Third Annual Report 2002).

Since a conservative estimate for the cost to produce a compact disc is roughly $3.50 (Roberts 2002) and that CDs are sold around $15.99 - 18.98 (Campbell 2000; Dominick 2002), one can see there is plenty of room for the industry to generate profits. The actual expense of manufacturing a CD is more likely to be less than a dollar per unit. Given that the cost of manufacturing a CD is quite inexpensive and the average retail cost of a CD is roughly $15.99, where does all of the money go?

DISTRIBUTION OF PROFITS MADE FROM COMPACT DISCS:

$4-5 Recording Label Profits
$3-4 Distributor and Store Profits
$1-2 Promotion and Advertising
$1-2 Designing and Packaging
$1-2 Recording and Studio Costs
$1-2 Miscellaneous-shipping, musician's fees etc.
$.50-1.50 artist's Royalty
(Campbell 2000)

Record companies reap the highest profit from music sales (close to four dollars on a typical CD), but along with the musical artist, also bare the expenses of manufacturing, packaging, design, advertising and promotional costs (Campbell 2000). More than 95 percent of all musicians who receive advances do not recoup them through recording sales (Campbell 2000). In addition, artists make a general royalty rate of 9 to 12 percent per CD sold (Dominick 2002). Because the industry focuses on a small group of artists with potential to cross-promote throughout the industry's various media holdings, most of the income generated by the industry is disproportionately divided going to a small group of musicians. Fewer then thirty artists sell more than a million CD copies a year, while maybe 250 will sell ten thousand copies (Dominick 2002).

While it is quite evident most musicians make very little money from CD sales and wealth is becoming more and more polarized toward the industry, upper management appears to profiting quite well. For example, EMI's Chairman recently made $997,249 while Chairman and CEO of EMI Music publishing made $5,248,774 ("EMI Group" 2003). Warner Music Chairman Tom Whalley also made $2.2 million and "earned" a $3.5 million bonus in 2003 (Christman 2004c). Their salaries do not appear to be feeling the so-called negative economic effects of file sharing.

CONGLOMERATE OWNED INDY LABELS AND GLOBALIZATION

All of the Big 4 companies own several smaller independent, or "indy" labels. As one can see in chart 3d, Sony owns Columbia, Epic, as well as other record companies. Warner Music Group (Time Warner) owns Atlantic, Word Entertainment, and Rhino in addition to other labels. Universal Music Group (Vivendi/Universal) owns A&M, Mercury, and Geffen. Bertlesmann Music Group (Bertlesmann), the German transnational, also owns Arista, BMG, and RCA, while EMI's assets include Capital and Virgin records.

CHART 3: RECORD LABEL INVESTMENT AND OWNERSHIP

WARNER MUSIC GROUP

Antone's	Desert	Lava	The Music
Aquemini*~	Storm*~	Luaka Bop	Label~
Asylum	Discovery	Mammoth~	Tommy
Atlantic	East West	Maverick	Boy*~
Records	American	Nonesuch	Top Dog*~
Big Beat	Electra	Pyramid~	Warner
Blackbird~	Elementree~	Quest~	Brothers
Blitzz~	Fishkin ~	Reprise	Records
Celtic	Flavor Unit*~	Resound	Warner/
Heartbeat~	Giant	Rhino~	Chappell
Che~	Igloo~	Sire	Music Inc
Curb	John Dough	Slash	
	Kinetic	Sub Pop	

EMI DISTRIBUTION

Angel Records	Doggystyle	EMI Latin~	Pangaea
Anise~	Records*~	EMI Records	Priority*~
Blue Moon	Global Pacific	Ensign~	Roswell~
Blue Note	I.R.S. Records	Jobete Music~	Virgin
Capitol	Java~	Manhattan~	Records
Records	EMI	Mesa	
	Christian~	Netwerk	

VIVENDI/UNIVERSAL

40 Acres and a
Mule
A&M Records
Abkco
Records
Aftermath*
Almo
Antilles
Attic
Bloodline*~
Blue
Capricorn
Cargo
CGI~
Cherry
Entertainment
~
Chronicles
City of
Angels~
Decca
Def Jam*
Def Squad*~
Deutsche
Gramm

DreamWorks
Eleven~
Flawless*~
Flip*~
Flyte Time~
Fort Apache
Geffen
Records
GTSP~
H.O.L.A.
Records~
Hollywood
Records~
House of
Blues
Imaginary
Records~
Impact
Interscope
Island Records
Kedar
Entertainment
L'Oiseau
Lil' Man
Load~

Mammoth~
Margaritaville
Records
MCA
Mercury
Mercury/
Nashville
Mercury/
Curb*
MoJazz
Mojo
Motown
Murder Inc.*~
Narada
Nothing
Records
Outpost
Pallas~
Phillips
Classics
Point Music
Polygram
Latino
Pure
Radio Active

Rebound
Rising Tide
Entertainment
River North
Roadrunner~
Rocafella*
Scratchie~
SpunOut*~
Step Sun
The Label*~
Timbaland's
Beat Club*~
Tack Factory~
Trauma
Triloka
True North
Twism
Twisted~
Underworld*~
Universal
Music
Uptown
Verve Group
Win

SONY MUSIC

550 Music
American Recordings
Aware*
Big Cat~
C2
Caviant
Chaos~
Columbia B'way
Masterworks
Columbia/ Nashville
Columbia Records
Crave~
Creation
Crescent Moon~
Epic Records
Essential Classics
Facility
Flip

Foodchain
Great
Performances
Hall of Fame*
Higher
Ground
Hoppoh
Immortal~
Independiente
Jersey
Legacy
Lifestyle
Loud
Lucky Dog
Masterworks
Heritage
MJJ~
Mosh~

Myrra~
New
Deal~
Okeh
Ovum*~
RocBlock/
Ruffhouse
Ruffhouse
*~
Ruthless*~
SEON
Skint*~
Slam Jamz
So So
Def*~
Sony
Classical

Sony Discos
Sony Latin~
Sony Records
Sony Square~
Sony
Tropical~
Sony Wonder
Soundtrax~
Stone Creek~
Trackmasters~
Tri-Star
Music~
Undertainment
*~
Vivarte
Word*~
Work
Yab-Yum

BMG LABELS (now part of Sony)

Arista Records	Flipmode*~	RLG Record	Windham Hill
Bad Boy	J Records	Label Group	Group
Records*	LaFace	Nashville	Wyclef
BMG	Records*	Time Bomb	Records
Classics/RCA	Melisma	Records	Zomba Group
Victor	Records~	Wicklow	(eighteen
BMG US	RCA Music	Records	labels)
Latin	Group		

* Indicates a joint venture/equity deal
~ Indicates a non-union-signatory label
Chart 3; Source: Kelley 2002; Roberts 2002.

Figuring out how independent labels are connected to the Big 4 is often difficult to accomplish. In most cases, labels are considered "independent" or "indy" if they are distributed though independent networks rather than through a major distribution company. This gets shady because a label can be partially owned by a major, but still be considered an indy because it goes though an "independent" distributor. On the other hand, an independent label that is distributed through a major will be considered a major label. In addition, major labels often form "spin-off" labels, but send their music through major and independent distribution networks, even though the label refers to itself as an independent. Additional major labels may purchase only part of an existing independent label and continue to send the records through an independent or a major distributor. The definitions become even more blurred when major labels own all or half of indy distribution networks such as Sony's purchase or RED distribution, EMI's interest in Caroline Distribution and Warner's partial purchase of ADA distribution (Roberts 2002).

The Big 4 are increasingly outsourcing expenses to smaller labels in order to save money. This trend follows suit with other corporate activity. The location of corporate activity in other industries, such as apparel, is dynamic, meaning static physical locations are now low less likely to exist (Korzeniewicz 1993). Limited term leases for certain manufacturing areas or overnight "sweatshops" may pop up anywhere in order to minimize costs. Appelbaum and Gereffi (1994) note economic activity can include contracting labor in areas within a country where wages are lower than in other manufacturing areas. These activities may then cease existing in a few weeks or months given the end of the contract agreement. Nonetheless there is a general trend in most industries to move to developing locations for cheaper labor, fewer taxes and minimal governmental regulations.

The music industry is following suit. However, instead of moving to other developing countries, the music industry has been moving to newer developing labels to outsource their work. There are additional gains to be made within this arrangement. By subcontracting production work to so-called "independent" record labels, the Big 4 are not bound by union contracts (Kelley 2002). Indeed, when the Big 4 own less than fifty percent of another company, they are not obligated to "ensure that the subsidiary honors the terms of the labor agreement" (Roberts 2002). This is why most majors own less than 50 percent of indy labels. This trend questions the so-called representation of the indys as "anti-establishment" given their role as non-union contractors (Roberts 2002). Within this scenario, the Big 4 do not need to pay professional musicians, which enables them to cut costs, similar to what other industries do by moving to developing countries. In addition, bands on some indy labels write their own music and perform it with their own band members. This aspect also aids the industry by cost cutting, although it appears to hurt business for professional musicians, as well as limit royalty income for the labels.

In sum, the high level of industry concentration along with substantial investment in smaller indy labels appear to have negative consequences for musicians by polarizing wealth between manufacturers and laborers. According to Roberts (2002), the

> growing number of joint ventures, pressing and distribution deals, equity deals, production company contracts, and distribution deals between independent and major labels (and between independent and major distributors) is a good example of the increasing industry control and concentration of power among a small number of corporations at the top, coupled with the dispersed production among many smaller labels at the bottom of the industry. The increasing market share of indys thereby translates into decreasing bargaining power of professional musicians and their organizations.

These trends are part of post-Fordist, post-industrial production practices that date back to the 1970s. This period is also indicative of a declining commitment by the federal government to support labor and worker's rights (Roberts 2002).

ESTABLISHED MODES OF OPERATION

> "There's a lot less imagination at the [major] labels because they can't really afford to have too much imagination"
> —Kenny Meiselas, industry lawyer,
> (Butler 2005a)

Meiselas's quote suggests the Big 4 are taking fewer risks resulting from pressure to maintain profits for investors. Indeed, this pressure may supercede all other activities at the label. Because of pressure to increase profits resulting from recent sales declines, the music industry is trimming artist rosters while promoting fewer artists with shorter contracts and more promotional money behind them. The Big 4 are also relying on fewer production companies to create hit songs. In addition, new software is being used to screen out songs without "hit potential." These industry trends are also affecting retail stores through their decision to cut back on CD selections. These "standardized" modes of operation contribute to the kind of sounds and song structures consumers hear in pop-oriented mainstream music, as well as affect the diversity of products available to consumers. The sum of these trends does not fare well for consumers seeking a more diverse array of musical artists and sounds.

Several Big 4 companies have been slashing their artist rosters beginning in 1999. These changes mean fewer mainstream musical acts will be promoted by the Big 4 and few will reap the benefits from corporate promotion plans and synergy. For example, UMG dropped hundreds of artists while shutting down or folding its smaller labels into larger ones in 1999 ("Universal Music" 2003). Time Warner Music Group also trimmed its roster of artists in 2003 resulting from reported financial loses (Holson and Fabrikant, 2003). In addition, Warner Music International cut between 150 to 600 acts while other WMG affiliates also pared down their labels. When Atlantic and Electra merged, they also cut roughly 250 acts (Christman 2004c). Furthermore, Sony Nashville cut its artist roster in half for the company's four imprints: Columbia, Epic, Monument and Lucky Dog during spring of 2003 ("Sony Music Nashville" 2003). BMG also declined to renew contracts for artists around the globe in 2004. For example, in Germany, which is one of the world's largest music markets, BMG did not renew up-to 60 percent of its German artists because their CDs did not sell more than twenty-five thousand copies each. EMI also noted in April of 2004 it would continue to cut 20 percent of it's artists (Clark 2004). A few years later, EMI cut 400 acts from its roster ("EMI Group" 2003).

The drop in artist rosters has had a negative impact on the total number of new releases during the first few years when the music industry was complaining of losing money from file sharing. In 1999, there were 38,858 total releases (6,924 by majors and 31,933 by independent labels). The number decreased in 2000 to 35,516 total releases. There were 6,188 major releases and 29,328 releases by independent labels during this time (Christman 2001b). The total numbers continued to decline in 2001 to 31,734 releases (6,455 by the majors and 25,279 by independents), but increased slightly in 2002 to 33,443 (7,306 by majors and 26,137 by independents) (Christman 2003b).

It is important to note that reissues of old albums are also often categorized as new releases, which can further decrease the amount of releases by new artists. Although there were still 5,415 fewer new releases in 2002 than in 1999, labels increased their new releases during 2002 mostly by increasing reissues in order to maintain overall catalog sales. They also made more pressing deals with independents while more Latin artists were hitting the mainstream (Christman 2003b).

These drops also affect the percentage of discs being manufactured. According to Sean Smith, L.A.-based senior VP of sales and marketing for JVC Disc America, one of the world's largest disc replicating companies "Two years later [in 2001], you have probably 8 percent of the artists creating 80 percent of the required manufacturing; you have very few artists requiring big replication runs and less of a market that is spread evenly across a variety of replicators. You have a huge glut of capacity" (Walsh 2001).

Indeed, only a few major label artists end up selling the most music. For 2000, .35 percent of all albums sold in the U.S. accounted for more than half of all units sold. Three percent of total available albums in the U.S. accounted for more than four-fifths of all album sales. Of all albums released in 2000, the major labels accounted for 28.9 percent of all available albums, yet accounted for 83.4 percent of all sales. Independent labels made up 71.1 percent of all albums, yet only accounted for 16.6 percent of sales (Christman 2001b). The polarization of sales in the music industry appears to reflect the polarization of wealth between the rich and the poor in the United States and throughout much of the "developing" world. In both cases, there is a very small group that controls resources and benefits economically from their allocation.

The industry's strategy of releasing fewer artists is also affecting retail, which is exacerbating the trend toward an increasingly less diverse music market. While retailers are becoming more concentrated with a few chain or mass merchants controlling more market share, they are also becoming less likely to promote newer artists. This is unfortunate because most new artists become established in independent or regional chains, eventually making their way into chain stores. When independent stores are losing market share while chains and mass merchants are increasing their shares, the range of culture appears to diminish. Most mass merchandisers rarely consider stocking newer artists unless it appears as if they are about to become household names. For example, according to Billboard, Target chains only focus on ten new, or developing artists at any one time (Christman 2002). Mass merchants are increasing their share of the music market because businesses like Wal-Mart continue to build new stores all over the United States and the rest of the world. Wal-Mart's plans were to open 235 new stores in 2002, while Target planned to open 115 during the same time period (Christman 2002).

They can also increase their market share by offering exclusive music unavailable in other stores. Some record labels were providing chain stores and mass merchants with differently issued CDs containing exclusive tracks early in 2000. Although temporarily halted, these product advantages were available at Target, Best Buy, and Wal-Mart (Christman 2002). In other cases, such as with the Rolling Stones, agreements have been made to exclusively sell new releases at Best Buy, which meant there was only one retail store that would stock the new CD for a certain period of time.

Because retail outlets are directly affected by the trends set by the industry, stores are now stocking fewer CDs while increasing the presence of other product lines in their shelves, such as DVDs, video games, and electronic products, which bring in higher profit margins (Christman 2003a). Tower records recently began selling more electronic devices in its stores, which in many cases meant replacing space originally allocated for CDs in order to provide twenty to thirty additional square feet of floor space for electronics. Best Buys' purchase of Musicland also moved more electronics products in

Musicland chains, while it also made its competitors note they would need to stock up to 30 percent fewer music titles to make way for more consumer electronic goods as well (Hardy 2000c).

The major labels are expected to continue the trend of selling only the most mainstream artists in order to achieve successful cross-promotional revenue levels ("Why Experts" 2003). The industry makes substantial profit off of older bands because they don't need as much advertising to "break" them into commercial culture (Leeds 2003). As a result, the Big 4 continues to re-issue older albums people already know of, which cuts into the likelihood that newer releases will garner additional promotion. Indeed, today's music industry is less concerned with the physical production of music, meaning the search for new artists, new sounds, or nurturing of talent, than with the marketing and distribution of existing stars (Kelley 2002). This makes good business sense given that CD sales mostly fund music industry components such as marketing and copyright divisions anyways (Dolfsman 2000). Selling well-known artists is a self-support mechanism generating assurances that sales will be able to sustain various industry divisions. This appeases stock holders, but also limits cultural diversity.

The reports of these industry trends echo within the academy and private sectors as well. According to Bruce Greenwald, professor of finance at Columbia Business School, the music industry is likely to sign even fewer artists in the future as a result of financial loses during 2000–2002 (Holson and Fabrikant 2003). Another media specialist at McKinsey & Company noted "Revenues today can't support such a broad number of releases . . . we are likely to see the big recording companies focus their bets more" (Holson and Fabrikant 2003). These trends negatively impact cultural diversity given newer artists of lesser stature will be sidelined. They will need to learn how to promote, sell, and direct market their material themselves. Ultimately, when so few firms control the majority of the music promoted around the world, the spectrum of available culture becomes limited. Indeed, according to Moshe Adler, an economist at Columbia University, "money is made by reducing diversity" (Mann 2000).

POP MUSIC PRODUCTION TEAMS

In addition to fewer artists, less diversity, more promotional money behind well-known artists, and the cut backs of CD selections in retail stores, it appears as if fewer people are now writing, making and producing pop music, which is the most likely kind of music to be advertised and cross-promoted. In other cases, the Big 4 are only promoting the artists who gave them the often lucrative rights to their performance royalties. This means the Big 4 are more inclined to promote acts based on ownership of royalties (see chapter 4 for a more detailed description of this process). Instead of going out and exploring new talent, Big 4

A&R teams are increasingly relying on a small number of production teams to write and produce pop music. This is because they have been successful in the past with creating top selling songs. The Big 4 are more likely to commission music to the teams, which then provide acts with entire packages minus vocals, or for some acts, write music together with the artist (Pride 1999).

The best-known examples of production teams that create pop music include Metro Productions and Cheiron. U.K.-based Metro Productions wrote and/or produced tracks for Cher, Tina Turner, Lionel Richie, Enrique Iglesias, French star Lara Fabian, Diana Ross, Point Blank, Jamie Lee, Cheri Amore, and others. Sweden's Cheiron wrote for and/or produced Dr. Alban, Ace of Base, Robyn, 3T, Britney Spears, 'N Sync, Backstreet Boys, Five, Bon Jovi, as well as others. Other production teams include Dreamhouse and Soul Power Productions, with the later having wrote or produced tracks for Toni Braxton, Whitney Houston, Brandy, Brownhouse, Monica, and others (Pride, 1999).

When four record companies that control roughly 80 percent of the world's music rely on a select few production teams, commercial pop music will end up sounding homogenized to a certain extent. Producers and writers not only create and arrange music, but they also shape the sounds of the instruments and effects. They are also the people who often tell performers what to sing about and how to do it. With fewer labels owning more music produced by fewer ears and minds means that cultural diversity becomes limited due to standardized industry modes of operation.

In addition to hearing more and more artists produced by the same production teams, consumers may begin to hear similar musical structures, patterns and melodies within the heavily promoted commercial music they hear. The music industry, as well as some radio stations are now using software that "filters out" songs not entailing features of hit songs during the past few decades.

HIT SONG SCIENCE SOFTWARE

As of 2003, all Big 4 labels in the United States and the U.K. have been using software called "Hit Song Science" (HSS) developed by Polyphonic HMI to determine the "hit potential" of music prior to its release ("Major Labels" 2003). The software analyzes the beat, harmony, pitch, octave, and other patterns in new songs, which are then compared to previously released hit songs in order to gauge the potential of the new music.

This invention will affect music culture on at least three different levels. First, at the top level, labels will be more likely to promote songs that have "hit potential" based on the computer program. On the second level, music producers will be more likely to gear their music to the software, while radio stations appear to use similar software putting them on the third level. Music will be tested, analyzed, and filtered in a three-stage process before it arrives on the radio and in retail stores. Ultimately, these trends stifle the creation of new music structures and melodies, and will probably further decrease the creativity and spectrum of artists and culture within the music industry.

On the first level, labels will be more likely to promote artists that fit into the technology's definition of "successful." Songs that have "hit potential" according to Polyphonic's software will be cross-promoted with financial backing given the database's historical track record with success. On the second level, music producers will be more likely to cultivate and create music to fit into structures and melodies that the program deems successful. Therefore producers who want to make a name for themselves or increase their salaries will be more likely to conform to what the industry wants based on the computer program.

On the third level, radio stations will be likely to further filter music based on additional technologies in order to base selections on commercial potential. Broadcasters already speed up songs or compress them altering the original format and sound of the music in order to make more room for commercials (Eisenberg 2003). According to Scott Shannon, morning DJ and program director for New York's WPLJ, "Radio stations are a lot more selective about which songs they play now. It's gotten to be a very researched business. There's so much testing going on and computer [analyzing] of what songs people like" (Huckman, 2003).

RADIO FOR SALE?

Besides the use of new technology, the Big 4 also manipulate the music consumers hear on the radio via an additional three-tired process. First, the Big 4 pay promoters (who also pay station fees) to push Big 4 songs on radio. Second, labels also pay to have their songs aired during advertising time, while last, the illusion of popularity based on chart success further aids the promotion of various musical acts, as well as consumer purchasing decisions.

The first stage of this process has independent promoters paying radio station fees, which often exceed $100,000 (Leeds 2004b). Knowing who paid the station's fees, the stations then "consider" playing the music given to them by the promoters. For every song played on the air, or entered into play lists, the promoters then bill the Big 4 labels, which costs them tens of millions of dollars per year (Leeds 2004b). In a 2003 speech by FCC commissioner Jonathan S. Adelstein, he noted reports that promoters were paying some radio stations up-to $400,000 to "consult" on what should be played ("FCC Should Probe 'Payola'," 2003).

In the event the first stage of radio manipulation is not effective, or to accompany the technique, a growing number of labels now buy advertising time through "spot buys" on small to medium sized radio chains and simply have the djs play their music (Garrity 2004b). This is the second stage by which radio is manipulated by monied interests. Sometimes the labels' singles are played hundreds of times per week, often after midnight when advertising is much cheaper. Nonetheless, these "spot buys" obviously help propel singles on the charts, which then generate more "buzz." Basically, labels can now buy their way to the charts. Why should the public worry about payola, when advertising simply takes over this function in the radio business.

Indeed, music charts can be seen as corporate constructs often orchestrated by finance more than public appeal. It doesn't even matter anymore if people hear or like the singles. According to one major-label VP, "It's not about selling records, its simply about getting spins" (Garrity 2004b). As a result of this manipulation, more than 25 percent of all singles on the Mainstream Top 40 are supported by "spot buys," or similar funding activities with labels spending between $3,500-4,500 to buy up to forty-two spins (Garrity 2004b).

Once the songs hit the charts, additional exposure occurs based on the publicity generated from their promotion. This is the third process by which radio is manipulated. Charts also trigger purchasing decisions, which may then lead to more demand for certain songs to be played on the radio. Ironically enough, if the Big 4 also own the rights to the music, then they make additional revenue from royalties garnered via radio airplay, which is considered a public performance. In essence, those who put money in the jukebox get to hear the tunes they paid for. In this case, they can also receive money for playing them as well.

For the public that complains about the music played on the radio as sounding homogenized, they may now have a good argument in support of their claims given the trend toward fewer artists, fewer production teams and the use of computer programs. According to Tracie Reed, vice president Polyphonic's North American office, after having loaded every song from Billboard's top 30 over the last five years into hit song science, "lo and behold, they all had something in common" (Strauss 2003). To be fair, it is possible that music could be improved as a result of the computer program. However, one can also argue that the range of diversity has been limited as a result of these trends. Unfortunately, the industry's reliance on software and marketing research to determine the "hits" may be a factor in the decreasing popularity of the music being produced given the decline in sales.

The trend toward using software programs based on previously profitable music suggests other kinds of music not in radio station or major labels' databases do not have value. The software appears based on what music sounds like, not what the messages are about. In addition, different kinds of music – possibly non-western or non-pop music, could be just as successful if they were in radio and "hit potential" data bases. For example, Radio K International, the international music show at the University of Minnesota, is the most popular of all programs on the station possibly because it plays non-Western music without software or marketing databases that determine the "hits."[1]

CONCLUSION

This chapter described the Big 4 companies that own and control most of the world's music. Because owners influence the music people hear, as well as where and how they listen to it, understanding media ownership helps contextualize recent developments affecting consumers and culture. As a result, this chapter described media conglomeration as related to the music industry, as well as the industry's market share, consolidation, recent revenue and ownership patterns. Because of conglomeration, the Big 4 are able to easily cross-promote their own content, as well as save money on production costs. Finally, the established modes of production resulting from ownership patterns were also investigated. The music industry has been trimming artist rosters, promoting fewer artists, relying on fewer production companies, using new software to determine hit songs, as well as manipulating radio content. These trends also affected retail stores through their decision to cut back on CD selections. As a result of these recent developments, this chapter argued pop music is becoming increasingly less diverse due to industry concentration and pressure to increase revenue.

NOTES

1. Interview with Paul Harding, veteran radio dj at Radio K at the University of Minnesota, Minneapolis. August, 2002.

CHAPTER 4

CONGLOMERATION AND HYPER-COMMERCIALISM

As discussed in the previous chapter, the music industry is changing its modes of operation by cutting artists rosters, focusing on fewer producers and by using new technology to determine "hits." It is also using its other media holdings to increase promotion. This chapter focuses on how the music industry is dramatically increasing the commercialization of musical artists through advertisements and products. It also examines how this is affecting musicians and culture. It first discusses the modes of promotion popularly utilized within the industry including cross-promotion within and across media and products, co-branding between companies and circular marketing tactics such as "price points" and "cleans" that attempt to measure the degree of media exposure for a given product and subsequently create hype.

Second, this chapter explores how cross-promotion not only benefits companies by reducing advertising costs, but also produces steady and reliable revenue in the form of royalties garnered from publishing rights held by music companies. In this scenario, more exposure yields additional profits for companies holding the publishing rights to music, which makes cross-promotion a handsome prospect, especially when corporations have the ability to cross-promote within their own conglomerate holdings.

Finally, this chapter addresses how this hyper-commercialism manipulates culture by reducing it into an advertisement for corporate conglomerates. Artists and their music become subjugated to the marketing demands of the handful of companies that determine which artists are granted viable exposure. In short, the hyper-commercialism sparked by conglomerate business warps music culture into an advertising blitz for corporations, while muddling the line between culture and commerce.

Ultimately, commercialism within the music industry is increasing for four reasons. First, with co-branding (where two companies advertise at the same time), advertising is now cheaper because the expenses can be shared between both businesses. This means that companies can double the amount of advertising without doubling their budgets. Second, increasing media conglomeration makes cross-promotion easier and cheaper given single ownership of several media outlets. Third, the Big 4 can make additional royalty revenue when their music is cross-promoted and advertised because they usually own the rights to the music. Finally, with the Internet as a potential distribution and promotional threat to the Big 4, the more advertising of Big 4 musical artists, the more likely they will be able to control their market share.

CROSS-PROMOTION

Musicians are now as likely to be on television or in movies as they are likely to be on the radio. Music and musicians are becoming ubiquitous throughout all media. Mike Dreese, CEO and founder of the Newbury Comics, a New England record-store chain, agrees with the increase in music marketing in new outlets. He sees the music industry following the Tiger Woods model of marketing where money can be made not just off music, but by tapping into endorsements, speaking engagements and various commercials. These commercials are forms of "co-branding," where two or more corporations advertise together through a single product. Co-branding is becoming increasingly popular with music. "The role of the record label is going to be as a venture capital brand-building organization. It'll be perfectly reasonable for them to approach the next Avrill Lavigne and say we'll give you a million dollars up front, but we want a revenue split of all future movies, concerts, endorsements and merchandise" ("Why Experts" 2003). Here, if one wants to become a household name through the promotional gatekeepers, one will have to do it through their terms. One way of building up a brand is to feature songs and musical artists in nearly every area imagined, from sports to movies, to chips to coffee chains like Starbucks to cell phones to the World Wrestling Federation (WWF).

BLOCKBUSTER PHENOMENON

One of the most obvious examples of cross-promotion within conglomerate media comes in the form of movies such as Jurassic Park or the Lion King. Here, conglomerates cross-promote films and characters in various outlets such as pay-per-view cable, video games, theme rides, toys, and comic books. The total number of licensed product lines for Jurassic Park approached one thousand in its first year of release (Shatz 1997).

The most obvious examples of conglomeration within the music industry come in the form of "boy" and "girl" bands such as 'N Sync, the New Kids on the Block, Backstreet Boys, or the Spice Girls. Jive records (co-owned by BMG Entertainment) was responsible for creating most of these successful bands. 'N Sync set a record by selling 2.4 million copies of their album "No Strings Attached" during its first week ("BMG Entertainment" 2003). The industry is developing these and other artists into "blockbuster" phenomenon by cross-promoting them in film, video games, through t-shirts, TV specials, cartoons, hats, pencils, school folders, posters, and food items. An expanding number of music-related projects are using merchandising licensing to the point where there was $110 billion generated from retail sales of licensed products in 1999. The manufacturers of these products paid a record $5.5 billion in royalties to rights owners in 1998 (Traiman 1999c).

One of the goals of promoting these sorts of bands is to tap into youth markets given their fair share of disposable income. The labels purposefully target younger audiences because they have decent purchasing power and are more apt to follow trends according to their age group characteristics. Preteen music consumers have become a driving force in the music industry, buying millions of music products while breaking acts that top 40 radio and MTV won't bother with. These nine to fourteen year-olds are worth some $260 billion per year in spending power (Taylor 2001). In fact, advertisers see younger people still living with their parents as three-way targets. First, advertisers can get the money they make from allowances or small jobs. Second, they can get their parents' money via the kids and third, they can hopefully earn future brand loyalty by targeting consumers at such an early age. Disney has been targeting both the two to five-year-old market as well as the six to eleven-year-old market with a number of new audio releases promoted through soft drink manufacturer Welch. In 2000, Walt Disney Records launched its massive "tween"-targeted (tween referring to the age group "between" children and teenagers) marketing campaign to promote the release of "La Vida Mickey" (McCormick 2000).

COMMERCIALS

Music used in commercials can come from labels co-owned or connected to the product in the commercial as well. One song used in a TV commercial can produce $45,000 to as much as several hundred thousand dollars for the label, artist and publishing company through licensing revenue and royalties (Traiman 2003a). For example, Celine Dion's $10 million contract with Epic records also featured her song 'I Drove All Night' in a series of Chrysler commercials. She was also working with Coty to launch her own fragrance "Celine Dion Perfumes" and was to be featured in a series of concerts at Caesars Palace in Las Vegas. Chrysler communication director Bonita Coleman Stewart said "'I Drove All Night,' which we chose as our signature song from her new album, is playing on 200 radio stations…That is our idea of an integrated partnership, where a consumer hears a song and also has a visual depiction of Chrysler. It pulls it all together for the consumer and mutually benefits Celine's record label" (Taylor 2003). Other artists are also performing for car manufacturer Mitsubishi. According to Pierre Gagnon, Mitsubishi Motors N.A. president and CEO, "The most powerful proof is when a DJ comes onto the radio and says, 'And now, the Mitsubishi song'" (Huckman 2003).

American Express also advertised with Sheryl Crow, Hummer with Ms. Jade, and Coke with the Counting Crows (Christman 2003a). Garth Brooks, the Black Eyed Peas, and Thalia have all starred in Dr. Pepper commercials. Faith Hill and Queen Latifah are also Cover Girl spokesmodels who appeared in print and TV ads. L'Oreal's TV ads featured members of Destiny's Child and Jennifer Lopez. Missy Elliot was also featured in Reebok advertisements, while Sugar Ray's McGrath has been featured in TV ads for Candie's and Levi's. Kraft teamed with Aaron Carter, Coors Light with Dr. Dre, and the Gap has also featured a number of musical artists in its commercials (including the aforementioned Missy Eliot of Reebok fame) (Hay 2002). The list is ever expanding.

One of the best examples where one can find cross-promotion and co-branding/advertising in the conglomerate music industry is within Sony. They have been successful in making money by promoting their own music in their own commercials. For example, in one of Sony's commercials for a Sony electronics product, Epic Records (owned by Sony) music act Macy Gray sings a cover of Aerosmith's "Walk this Way" (Newman 2004b). Ironically, Aerosmith also have music on the Sony Label. Here, the public is exposed to three commercials conveniently packed into one.

Given it's capabilities to vertically integrate, Sony may be able to film the commercial in it's studios on it's own equipment, then write off advertising costs as a business expense. Sony receives publicity for it's electronics product through the commercial and the exposure will help promote Macy Gray, who is ultimately a Sony artist, and it rejuvenates an old song from Aerosmith's catalog, which also has music on Sony labels. According to *www.fretplay.com*, Sony also owns the copyright to the song "Walk this way." Therefore, Sony will not only bring in public performance revenue by airing the song it owns on television and radio, but it will likely make more money by exposing Macy Gray to a larger audience assuming it will purchase Macy Gray CDs. The present system is wonderfully regulated in favor of conglomerate profits. At the same time, how could anyone point out Sony for taking advantage of the system? Interestingly enough, commercials are not the only place where musical artists affiliated with conglomerate labels are featured. Several of these musicians, as well as their music, are also prominently displayed in television shows and in movies.

TELEVISION SHOWS AND MOVIES

Again, cross-promotion of conglomerate artists helps with exposure and brings in additional revenue from public performance royalties and sales of downloads, hardcopy CDs, DVDs and other items. Indeed, EMI Music Publishing film soundtrack division VP Alison O'Donnell noted people who see films and TV shows often want to purchase the music by the musicians they see and hear (Bessman 2003). If exposure helps musicians sell CDs and if companies bring in performance revenue, then profit-minded business people would be fools not to jam pack movies and television shows with their own music acts. In some cases, like the Sony commercial, the public sees incest-driven culture. In other cases, the musicians may not be directly signed to the company that is airing the television show or program. Nonetheless, the proliferation of conglomerate musical artists on conglomerate owned television channels and movies no doubt benefits the industry much more than it contributes to a diverse and vibrant musical culture.

The list of famous musicians from large corporate labels on television is almost endless, but here are a few examples. In 2004, Queen Latifah was to be featured in UPN's sitcom "Whot," Jessica Simpson starred on an ABC variety show, Ashlee Simpson appeared on an MTV reality show, Hilary Duff worked out a sitcom development deal with CBS, while Method Man and Redman were developing a Fox sitcom, and Britney Spears signed to be on an ABC Family Channel TV movie (Hay 2004b). However, not all of these programs were successful and some were cancelled.

Other shows on television are about musical groups themselves. For example, CBS had a television show featuring contestants hoping to be the next singer of pop group INXS. CBS was in a good position to do this because Viacom owned them, which had holdings in cable through MTV and VH-1, as well as through radio with Infinity Broadcasting. CBS then cross-promoted this show and band through its conglomerate holdings to increase revenue through royalties and sales.

However, CBS and Sony are not the only companies that cross-promote based on their holdings. EMI, although it doesn't have as many conglomerate arms as Sony, also has similar agreements in which soundtracks are limited to EMI musical material. For example, movies such as Bad Boys II, Lost In Translation, and Lizzie McGuire all had songs from EMI's catalog (Bessman 2003). In other cases, sometimes publishers will put a previously unreleased song in a movie in to lure fans. MPL publishing (owned by Paul McCartney) did this by placing the previously unreleased McCartney tune "Love for You" in the movie "The In-Laws" (Bessman 2003).

Besides music and television shows, more and more artists are also cross-promoted in movies. Eve appeared in blockbuster movies Barbershop and XXX, while Jennifer Lopez was recently featured in a film by Sony Pictures Entertainment, the sister company of Sony Music Entertainment which is her music label (Benz 2001b). Sony's film arm often adds music from its music arm. For another example, in the soundtrack for Spider-Man 2, Sony released eleven different versions of the soundtrack worldwide to feature select Sony artists ("Weaving 'Spider-Man' Music" 2004).

Another example where we see incestuous corporate activity masquerading as innocent fun is in the television show 'American Idol.' In a nutshell, most of the music contestants sing on "American Idol" is determined by music publishing executives. The contestants are usually allowed to choose amongst songs in EMI's catalog. EMI also sponsors theme shows based on EMI-heavy genres. "One of the first we did was a Motown show, because we publish the Jobete catalog" said O'Donnell, EMI Music Publishing VP (Bessman 2003). EMI also has a similar presence in "American Bandstand" and "American Dream" TV shows.

Therefore, similar to the earlier mentioned Sony commercial, new and deep catalog songs are sung by contestants, which is arranged by companies who own the copyright to the music. The companies can reignite interest in the songs, as well as gain revenue from public performance royalties. But the money doesn't stop there. The exposure gained by the winning contestants sometimes allows them to record CDs and perhaps tour. In July of 2004, there were already eleven "American Idol" competitors that made the Billboard charts ("Another 'Idol' Hit" 2004). Here, their made-on-TV fame translated into to selling fairly large quantities of compact discs. The only drawback to selling lots of compact discs is that musical artists rarely make much profit from them. Most of the money gets siphoned to the Big 4.

The songs on CDs by American Idol contestants can often be older tunes, perhaps not well known to younger people. This is done on behalf of music publishers to "educate" younger people about these older songs so publishing companies can recycle profits generated from these tracks through performance royalties. Not only did the music publishers make money when the songs were hits several years ago, but because they still own the rights, why not repackage them and make money again. It's often easier to make more money by repackaging an old song or artist rather than by breaking a new and unknown song or artist.

Indeed, most teenagers aren't going out to track down "Heat wave" or "I heard it through the grapevine." However, if it's on an 'American Idol' contestant's CD they saw on television, it may be a bit more "cool." At the same time, very few consumers or viewing audiences know how this incestuous love affair works unless they follow music industry journals geared toward investors. It is also extremely unlikely that a mainstream journalist who wanted to create a news segment on horizontal cross-promotion in the culture industries would be supported by editors. Even if something like this did air in the mainstream news media, the journalist would probably be disciplined or possibly demoted. Unfortunately, the innocent fun that takes place on American Idol and American Bandstand adversely affects the diversity of U.S. culture and does a disservice to independent artists and musicians everywhere.

SPORTS

Besides television and film, music and musicians are increasingly being advertised in sporting activities. While we can see famous artists during important football games, viewers are seeing more and more musical artists during basketball games. Promotional spots for the NBA are now featuring artists from Big 4 labels and similar artists can now be heard in the NBA giant apparel store in New York (Bachelor 2003). BMG labels also made a joint venture with Showtime Network to promote musical acts with boxing events on the Showtime cable channel and on SET. Artists on the label will sing the national anthem while banners for additional BMG ads are featured on television (Bessman 1999). Finally, WMG has also linked a cross-promotional alliance with Chevrolet to plug its acts at NASCAR events. WMG's artists will appear on the actual racing cars, while TNT, a WMG-affiliated company, will feature these events in its TV coverage. Hootie and the Blowfish, Uncle Kracker, and several other artists are scheduled to be painted on the cars, as well as perform during the events (Garrity 2003c).

FAST FOOD RESTAURANTS, THEATERS AND SODA

Besides being featured as actual food, like "Rap Snacks," which consist of potato chips, popcorn, nachos and cheese curls featuring different UMG recording artists such as Mack 10, Baby, Master P and others on the bag, music is now featured in an increasing number of restaurants (Hall 2003). On occasion, fans will need to go to restaurants like McDonald's or Burger King if interested in exclusive artist material. McDonald's was the only place that sold a compilation of exclusive tracks and remixes by N'Sync and Britney Spears. Burger King also sold an exclusive live Backstreet Boys CD and video, while Spears recorded an exclusive song for Pepsi (Hay 2002).

Over one hundred Riese restaurants are also collaborating to promote music in Houlihan's, TGI Friday's, Dunkin' Donuts, Kentucky Fried Chicken, Pizza Hut, and Roy Rogers. Cuts from featured artists are played with five second announcements (during intros and outros) informing consumers about the artist and where they can purchase the music. In addition, monthly compilation CDs are displayed daily in the restaurants. Most of the artists are from UMG labels.

Each label pays $4,000 per track, which is played three times a day (Traiman 2001b).

In addition, labels also pay to have their music heard in various private places that see heavy traffic from large amounts of people. The United Artists (UA) Theatre Radio Network will play musical artists ten times a day in the 335 theater lobbies across the U.S. for $5,000 per song, per month. They can also be featured on their new video wall of multiple TV screens in 240 locations (Traiman 1999a). Rachel Farris's label, Big 3 Records, is also placing mini-CDs in the lids of soft drink cups at 530 movie theaters and a few theme parks around the United States. The theaters will show a three-minute video of Farris before the featured movies begin ("Promo Uses CDs" 2003). The trend toward promoting music with soda and other products appears to be exploding around the world. Pepsi used Columbian singer Shakira in an enhanced CD campaign throughout South America and Spain, while contact lens maker Acuvue promoted an enhanced CD with exclusive footage and song mixes by Enrique Iglesias ("Promo Uses CDs" 2003). Finally, Anderson Merchandisers, one of the largest magazine wholesalers, which also recently purchased into Liquid Audio, had plans to cross-promote downloaded music with various magazines and beverages such as Coca Cola. Consumers could acquire stickers on soda cans for free downloads, or receive a free download by purchasing specific magazines. "This will strategically position retailers to participate in the industry's legitimate downloading future" noted an industry executive (Holson 2003b). Sony also worked a deal with McDonald's Corp to give away free downloads, while most other digital online music services have joint ventures with various consumer brands like United Airlines and Pepsi Co. ("Napster Gives Away" 2004). The point with giving away free downloads was to move consumers online to purchase music through digital downloads where the music industry can make higher profits.

PRICE POINTS AND CLEANS

The more an artist is cross-promoted in various media outlets, the better chance the artist will be promoted within retail stores. The invention of "price points" aids this process. "Price points" consist of a numerical system, which in theory, is supposed to parallel demand for a product. For example, TV appearances, movie appearances and commercial appearances by artists are given a certain quantity of points based on public media appearances. Even when there is a question on the TV show "Who Wants to be a Millionaire" about a recent Beatles reissue album, that disc is likely to receive "price points" for its appearance on national TV. These points are then supposed to indicate if the product will be more likely to sell in larger quantities. Products with higher price points are more likely to be promoted in retail stores, usually through placement, giveaways and posters.[1]

Besides price-points, the invention of "cleans" can also help promote various artists as well. "Cleans" exist at the distribution level of the music industry. They are products such as CDs, cassettes, Lps or singles that are not defined as promotional items, and their bar codes are not "punched," meaning they are for sale. Labels may send a box of free CDs as "cleans" with a page of $.99 cent stickers, as well as a poster promoting the product to be displayed next to the cash register. The labels will then tell the store to do whatever it wants with them. This means that stores can earn additional revenue if they decide to sell the products. What is important with this scenario is when consumers purchase a bar-coded CD for a dollar, it is scanned into the "Sound Scan" computer software. If a retail chain scans a large quantity of "cleans" into Sound Scan, it will appear as if an artist is in high demand. The labels then contact radio stations to try and convince them to play whatever song was on the $.99 CD single.

Here, labels with promotional power can create the impression that an artist is becoming quite popular with the public. Once the "clean" is aired on the radio, then sales usually increase as a result of exposure on a mass level. According to one study, just over a quarter of people aged 35 and older report purchasing a CD after hearing a single on the radio ("Declining Music" 2003). Unfortunately, Sound Scan is also not the most accurate indicator of sales given that numerous independent stores do not use it. To make up for these "lost" sales figures, Sound Scan may register three or more sales for every one CD purchased in larger retail centers. Even while independent retailers are disappearing, this approach assumes that consumers would purchase the same type of music from independent stores as in chain stores. By default, Sound Scan would then overestimate the number of CDs sold in favor of mainstream artists sold at chain stores.[2]

CONGLOMERATES AND PUBLISHING ROYALITES

Besides promoting music by price points and cleans, the economics of promoting music on television, radio and in movies also needs to be discussed in order to understand why an increase in appearances of music and musicians is taking place in our broadcast and visual media. According to Richard Rowe of Sony ATV (Sony's publishing arm), "… we have witnessed an almost total transformation of the music-publishing business. We are, as much as anything, in the film, television and advertising business these days" (Seay 2000).

The more a company cross-promotes, advertises or uses music on TV or in film, the more revenue it can generate from royalties. Indeed, publishing royalties come from a number of sources. They come from synchronization through audio, video, other media and print, or sheet music. In addition, they come from mechanical reproductions in the form of CDs, ringtones/tunes, and digital downloads. Royalties also come from public performances and broadcast/cable transmissions, meaning through radio, television, and other venues (Butler 2005b).

David Rezner, president of Universal Publishing notes "In the area of global synchronization, we have seen a growth of over 20 percent in the last year [1999] alone" (Seay 2000). The growth in "synchronization," where music is cross-promoted in various advertisements, media or events brought in a 30.9 percent rise in revenue in 1997 to $864.17 million (Lichtman 1999a). In fact, music publishing is so profitable that when Sony Music Group merged with BMG in 2004, the music publishing divisions were excluded because they are too valuable in terms of generating income through cross-promotion and advertising ("Sony Music-BMG Merger Sails" 2004).

The interesting part of the system is that cross-promotion doesn't have to occur within conglomerate corporations in order for money to be made. For example, a week after Time Warner let PBS rebroadcast a tribute concert to George Harrison, the sales of the DVD doubled (Levine 2004). Not only did Time Warner increase it's revenue from the public performance broadcast royalties, it also made more money from hardcopy sales after it aired the program. The important thing to note is that PBS is not owned by Time Warner.

However, conglomerates have an advantage over other record companies due to their ability to not only advertise their own products, but also to increase revenue through higher publishing profits. For example, Universal Music Group, with its roughly 25 labels, controls about one million copyrights in addition to independent music publisher Rondor Music ("Universal Music" 2003). BMG Entertainment also owns the publishing rights to more than 700,000 songs, ("BMG Entertainment" 2003) while Sony owns publishing rights through a joint venture with Sony Music Entertainment, Sony Music Entertainment Japan and Michael Jackson called Sony/ATV Music Publishing ("Sony Music" 2003). In addition, Warner Music Group has a publishing unit known as Warner/Chappell publishing, which holds the rights to more than a million songs ("Warner Music" 2003). Finally EMI, as the world's largest publishing arm, owns rights to over a million songs. It recently purchased music publisher Windswept Pacific for $200 million ("EMI Group" 2003). Owning publishing rights enables, among other things, the ability to make money from album sales. Actual bands, artists, or writers rarely possess the publishing rights to their music unless they own the label that is releasing it.

Money from royalties has been increasing. In 2004, royalty collection group BMI indicated its revenue and royalty distributions were the largest in the company's history. In fact, during 1995–2004, BMI's average growth rate was 9 percent, even when the music industry was complaining about lost revenue due to file sharing. For 2004, revenue grew to $637 million, while its royalty distributions grew to $537 million. Its 1986 revenue was only $189 million, while it's royalty distributions were only $162 million ("BMI Reports Record" 2004). Universal Music Publishing Group (UMPG) also saw its revenue shift from mechanical royalties in 1998 from 60 percent to 52 percent (Newman 2005). This suggests it's bringing in more money from public performances through commercial/TV and radio income. Its performance income rose from 21 percent to 25 percent, while its synchronization revenue grew from 10 percent to 14 percent (Newman 2005). From 2003–2004, it continued to see double-digit growth from synchronization income. Just to state the value of royalty divisions connected to or owned by larger conglomerate companies, Warner Music's publishing arm Warner/Chappell was valued at $700 million to $1 billion in 2003 ("Race to Merge" 2003). Given the Big 4's roster cuts, it is likely that most music-related income is coming from a much smaller group of well promoted musicians than in previous decades.

Indeed, because record labels own the publishing rights to music, which enables them to make additional money from public broadcasts, the more the Big 4 cross-promote within their own and other media holdings the more revenue they generate. Every time a song is played on the radio, in a movie, a commercial or in any public performance, music publishers can earn money if it is reported to a publishing association such as the American Society of Composers, Authors, and Publishers (ASCAP), Broadcast Music Incorporated (BMI), or other similar organization. These organizations were formed to issue licenses and to collect all due royalties "from three sources: the performance of songs, with recording artists receiving income based on the revenue made from the sale of their records; the sale of original music to publishers, and the subsequent performance royalties; and money paid to the publishers for their share of the sales and performances, usually split fifty-fifty between composers and publishers" (Eliot 1989; Shuker 2001). In theory, publishers and writers each make money when this occurs. However, in terms of radio play and royalties, many independent, college or community radio stations only submit a few play lists per year to ASCAP or BMI compared to corporate chains.

Unfortunately musical acts can hit national and international charts in college and community stations, even the top ten and still not receive a penny from public performance royalties based on radio airplay.[3] In fact, the radio stations that pay the most to royalty collection agencies such as BMI or ASCAP are the large corporate stations that ASCAP and BMI ask more frequently to report what they played. The big stations may also pay more fees to these agencies. However, these are the stations where music promoters are likely to pay their fees!

Community, public and college stations pay much smaller fees to royalty agencies and these stations are less likely to have promoters paying their fees, since they may operate more democratically and/or focus on lesser-known artists. ASCAP and BMI may only report one day worth of songs per year for these stations. So new and up-and-coming bands hoping to cash in on radio royalty payments due to their chart success on public, college or community stations should think twice before going on a credit card spending spree. It is likely they won't see a cent. Only music played on larger corporate stations, which usually consists of corporate pop, rap, country, or "alternative" music will see royalty payments, of which 50 percent or more will most likely go to the labels because they own the rights.

Even if musicians are supposed to get money from airplay, they may have to fight for it with their labels. It appears as if musicians are often responsible for pressuring the majority of Big 4 owned or affiliated publishing houses to get their earned royalty payments. For example, in 2004, New York State Attorney general Eliot Spitzer settled with the major U.S. record labels for $50 million in royalties. The labels were hoarding artists' royalties for years and were legally forced to hand over the money, but got away with keeping the interest accrued (Holland 2004).

At a time when the industry has been complaining about lost revenue while cutting back on artist rosters, revenue from publishing rights has remained stable and appears to be on the upswing. ASCAP reported an all-time high revenue of $668 million in 2003, which was an increase of 5.2 percent from the previous year (Horwitz 2004). Indeed, music publishing assets fetched high prices in 2003 (Benz, Christman, and Garrity 2003). These ancillary or secondary markets provide disproportionately large returns through licensing and revenue from copyright (Vogel 1994; Shuker 2001). Revenue from publishing rights have remained stable, their assets have been earning high prices and the industry has decreased the number of artists. These trends suggest the industry has increased its cross-promotion of music within media holdings while moving further into content generation. The industry appears to be redefining itself as content creators as a result of their push to increase revenue generated through publishing rights (Hardy 2003a). Besides increasing cross-promotion as an additional means of generating income, the labels are also increasingly eyeing up profits artists traditionally made in concerts, sponsorships and merchandise sales (Holson and Fabrikant 2003).

PUBLISHING RIGHTS AND PROMOTION

Another trend in the music business has labels promoting acts whose music is already written by label-connected or owned writers. Companies are becoming more likely to push artists who gave away their song writing rights to the label and to promote performers who sing company-owned songs. Labels can then expand their share of royalties into what would have normally gone to performers who wrote their own music. This means labels will get a higher percentage of the income generated from music sales, radio play and other exposure.

In fact, according to Co-Chairman of Atlantic Recording Group Craig Kallman, WMG now has "a mandate to be more collaborative" with Warner/Chappell Music Publishing (Newman 2004a). Another quote illustrates the desire for the talent seeking area of the industry to focus and promote more artists whose songs may already be owned by the publishing divisions. "We have mandated that our A&R departments focus more on artist development and catalog exploitation for our entire roster of writers" noted Les Bider, Warner/Chappell Music chairman/CEO (Bessman 2004). This trend also has important implications for cultural diversity. If publishing arms are suggesting who to promote based on who writes the music – meaning giving preference to music that is written by musicians who sold their rights to the company, then musical artists who write their own music and want to keep their music writing rights may end up sidelined.

Finally, the music industry is also beginning to see labels started and run by publishing executives. For example, Evan Lamberg, the VP of EMI Music Publishing in North America recently started E.V.L.A. Records Entertainment, which is a new joint venture with Atlantic Records. These trends suggest the public will hear more music by performers whose song writing rights are owned by the labels. This also suggests that decisions affecting mainstream culture are obviously economic decisions being driven by ownership, not talent or merit.

MUSIC CULTURE AND HYPER-COMMERCIALISM

Increasing coordination between labels, publishers and parent companies means that artists not only make music, they also have to sell themselves as a brand for their label. While the Internet may be able to challenge existing media institutions and systems of distribution (Shapiro 1999), the music industry is using both its conglomerate owners' media outlets and other non-affiliated outlets to produce better name recognition for its artists in order to assure threats to their media infrastructures will be minimized. The Big 4 parent companies have the power and capability to dominate cultural spheres with their immense vertical and horizontal holdings in radio, television, movies, magazines and newspapers.

Competition will be beat by the ability of one corporation to cross-promote and advertise its products against another, which will make survival for independent labels without massive conglomerate backing difficult. Simultaneously, more income will incur with increased promotion resulting from publishing rights associated with public performances and broadcasting. The ultimate result of this hyper-commercial atmosphere for consumers will be the further erosion of the fine line between art, free expression, and advertising. Music and musicians will be treated as commodities to be advertised for their conglomerate companies, while consumers may not be able to recognize the difference between commercials, TV shows, or movies.

The difference in the current marketing of musicians is that the major labels are negotiating the marketing deals based on their labels' interests. Prior to the past few years, musicians marketed themselves through various products, often under their own terms. Now, the major labels are negotiating the marketing deals based on their labels' terms. In many ways, this is a move toward branding music labels through the notoriety of musical artists. Although artists have the final say if they want to participate, the Big 4 conglomerates obviously have better contacts with the advertising world than do individual artists. This new arrangement appears to further submit the artists to the likings of their label, which means the label has more power in directing artists' public and commercial appearances.

CONCLUSION

This chapter focused on the increasing commercial nature of music by industry conglomerates. It noted music companies are using new and more creative methods to market their products, such as co-branding, which has the benefit of streamlining advertising expenditures. By using one product or outlet to market another, companies create more advertising exposure for less investment. Furthermore, this chapter noted companies also create revenue by collecting royalties from publishing rights, which can increase with promotion and advertising. Finally, increased commercialism further blurs the line between art and advertising in addition to cultivating an environment that subverts musicians and their music to the likes of the music industry. In essence, the increase in music commercialism is like an incestuous love affair between and within conglomerates, which turns culture into an advertisement for the corporate media industries.

NOTES

1. Interview with Daniel Sigelman, former music distributor in Minneapolis, Minnesota, August, 2002.
2. Ibid.
3. One of my bands was able to reach number 27 on the College Music Journal (CMJ) New World chart, number 3 on the Earshot International chart, as well as number 10 on the Chart Attack International chart. Although our music was registered through ASCAP, we never received any money from the airplay.

CHAPTER 5

CONGLOMERATION, HARDWARE AND REPEAT SALES

"At a time when other parts of the music business have been contracting, there's a high premium on finding new ways to generate sales."
—Paul Vidich, Executive Vice President for business development, Warner Music Group.
(Veiga 2003)

Besides increases in music advertising and cross-promotion throughout commercials, movies, as well as in fast food restaurants and soda cans, the music industry also stands to gain from CD burning and downloading through the sales of various electronic devices and software programs. In fact, music, electronic items and the software that enables them are increasingly owned by the same corporations. Moreover, because several of the Big 4 parent companies also manufacture computer and electronic equipment, the industry ironically makes money from what it argues is hurting sales. This chapter examines the connection between the Big 4 and various electronics and computer manufacturers. It looks at hardware such as CD burners, MP3 players and video games, as well as investigates new hardcopy media the music industry is hoping will replace standard CDs to gain additional sales. This chapter argues the industry hopes to spark multiple sales from one product by combining new hardware and communication services with exclusive music, as well as with the invention of new media forms. By dividing up exclusive media and access to music through new technologies and media, the industry hopes to conquer wallets and purses through the sales of these new products. It also hopes to spark another media replacement cycle, where consumers repurchase the same music in another format.

As a result of new technological advancements through compact discs, many consumers purchased the same music at least twice during the eighties and nineties. They first purchased releases on records and cassettes, then bought the same albums on CD thinking the new format was superior or easier to use. During this transitional period, the music industry's profits increased five-fold. Indeed, because of declining hardcopy music sales, the music industry recently changed its business plan to emulate the "2 sale" phenomenon it enjoyed during the last two decades. It is now reaching out to new technologies such as the Internet, video game consoles, and new audio formats. The goal is to force people to into buying additional hardware, software, or services that feature exclusive music, video or artist information. In addition, the industry is also introducing new products such as audio DVDs and SACDS (Super Audio Compact Discs) that require expensive hardware and are less likely to be pirated in the near future. In general, the industry hopes to accomplish three things with these inventions: first, generate multiple sales from one musical product, second, invent new media and converge different media which make copying difficult or impossible and third, increase revenue through cheaper distribution systems and formats through the Internet.

Their business plan appears to be working. Sales of music-oriented hardware are up. According to eBrain Market Research, portable headset CD players, single-play stand-alone component CD players, and multi-play stand alone component CD players exhibited the largest increase in household ownership from 2002 to early summer of 2003 ("CD Technology" 2003). In addition, Sean Wargo, senior industry analysis at Consumer Electronics Association stated in 2003 that "We are seeing strong and steady growth among CD-based and home theater audio categories" ("CD Technology" 2003). These home audio theaters are required if consumers want to play new media such as SACDs or audio DVDs.

CD BURNERS, CDRS AND SOFTWARE

Even though the music industry claims to lose money from CD burning, it also makes money from the very boogieman it blames for sales declines. Conglomeration can mean having two opposing players on the same team. For example, the music industry can complain about losing money from hardware that enables users to burn CDs, while producing hardware that copies CDs. It can also complain about MP3 files, while creating portable MP3 players. This way the industry benefits from scenarios it knows it cannot win if it only plays on one side. It cannot entirely stop copying or downloading for the moment, so why can't it make money from hardware sales when it may be losing money from hardcopy music sales? As long as profits are generated from the sum of conglomerate-owned divisions, why should inconsistency be a concern? As a result, most of the Big 4 parent companies sell a combination of hardware enabling CD copying, blank CDs, or software for copying.

For example, Matsushita, which owns part of Universal Entertainment, the parent company of Universal Music Group (UMG), also owns Panasonic, which manufacturers a number of DVD burners, CD burners, and portable devices that play music downloads. Both companies also sell DVD-Audio players ("Sony/Microsoft" 1999). In addition, Sony, Phillips, Iomega, JVC, Yamaha, Hewlett-Packard, Dennon, Pioneer, RCA, and TEAC also make CD burning hardware. Sony makes musical CDs that can be burned, as well as hardware to burn them. Japanese label Victor Entertainment is a subsidiary of JVC, which is also involved in CD replication. Dennon manufactures CD recorders and is part of Nippon Columbia, Japan's oldest record label. It recently established an American record label named Savoy. Philips owned Polygram Records while Matsushita, which also earns income from CD burning, owns the Victor Entertainment label and manufactures JVC disc burners (Walsh 2002). BMG owns RCA music group, while RCA also manufactures electronic hardware enabling CD burning. In addition, EMI is connected to Japanese electronics company, Toshiba, through its venture in Toshiba-EMI, which is 55 percent owned by EMI and 45 percent owned by Toshiba (McClure 2000). Toshiba makes a number of audio and computer devices that also burn and copy musical discs. Finally, blank discs are manufactured by companies including Maxell, Mitsui, Sony, Fujifilm, EMTEC, Apogee, TDK, HHB and Quantegy (Walsh 2002). At least one Big 4 company, Sony, is involved in producing blank discs. According to the International Recording Media Association (IRMA), worldwide sales of recordable CDs reached 3.7 billion in 2001. These CDs are taxed by several countries around the world with the money going to the Big 4.

The Big 4 are also buying into CD burning software companies such as Roxio and RealNetworks. EMI forged an alliance with Roxio, while UMG and Sony also own stocks in the company. Roxio claims to have a share of over 70 percent of the global market for CD burning products (Garrity 2001d). AOL and BMG are also connected to software company RealNetworks, which enables CD burning among other digital services.

MP3 PLAYERS

Money associated with music is also being made in other hardware divisions that manufacture MP3 players. MP3 players are portable electronic devices that allow consumers to play digital audio files. The concept is similar to portable cassette players or CD players, but the content is digital. The market for MP3 players has also increased substantially since their introduction during the 1990s. Worldwide revenues are expected to reach nearly $44 billion by 2007, representing a five-year compound annual growth rate of 30 percent ("Compressed Audio" 2003). The idea with MP3 players is to converge two technologies in order to make one product more appealing and functional for consumers while assuring the content and hardware do not enable "illegal" copying or transferring.

Most Big 4 companies are involved in the production of portable MP3 players. For example, Matsushita, which owns part of UMG's parent Universal Entertainment, makes portable electronic devices that play downloads ("Sony/Microsoft" 1999). Apple, which also owns an online distribution music service, makes MP3 players, while Sony makes them as well. Finally, RCA, which is connected to BMG, makes them while Panasonic, connected to UMG, also manufactures MP3 players.

Here is how hardware, corporate ownership and cross-promotion can often work. Roc Digital company makes a line of MP3 players called the Rocbox. One of the co-owners of Roc Digital planned to put images of the MP3 players in artist videos in his label, place tags promoting his clothing on them, as well as give consumers exclusive bits of music from the Roc-A-Fella label (Hansell 2004a). Fans of Roc-A-Fella recording artists would then have to buy the MP3 players in order to hear the exclusive music. This is also good for the parent label concerning tie-ins. Roc-A-Fella is part of Island Def Jam Music Group of UMG, which is owned by Vivendi Universal.

Other hardware interests are also jumping in the ring as well. Hewlett-Packard offers exclusive designed tattoos featuring UMG's latest releases to place on Apple's iPod ("HP Brings Digital Music To The Masses" 2004). Finally, Napster, which is owned by Roxio Inc., is so desperate to compete with Apple's iPods that it was giving away Rio Chiba Sports (portable MP3 players) for everyone who subscribed to Napster in 2004. The subscription service was valued at $119.40 at the time ("Napster Gives Away" 2004). Apple dominates the portable digital music player market with selling well-over 50 percent of all MP3 players.

VIDEO GAMES

Besides making hardware to burn music onto CDs, as well as manufacture MP3 players, the conglomerate music industry is also converging music with video game hardware. The goal is to not only cross-promote artists in games, but to also spark additional sales by offering exclusive music and artist-related content. Hardcore fans, or people who want access to new music releases, will now have to purchase video game consoles and new video games. Additional products for brand-specific consoles are also needed for purchase in order to enable music to be heard through larger speaker systems. Consumers now have to purchase their way through a series of "locks" in order to access music-related material and content.

Music and video games are converging because the market for video game consoles and the games themselves is worth more than $9 billion a year, with sales for Nintendo's GameCube console and Microsoft's Xbox going up roughly thirty percent each during 2002. Sales of additional video game consoles are also up ("Death of the Disc?" 2003). Sony's PlayStation 2 went up twenty-four percent during the same time period as well (Holloway 2003a). Therefore the music industry is moving into one of it's conglomerate parent's most profitable arms.

There are additional game-oriented products that are converging music with video games. One recent game-oriented invention called "SongPro" is a two-inch cartridge that can download music to be played on a Game Boy (Marriott 2003). SongPro includes a 32-megabyte Flash memory card, headphones, music management software, and a U.S.B. line to enable one to link up with any Internet-connected computer for music downloads. Song lyrics, CD cover art, and liner notes can be downloaded from SongPro's Web site, however, its technology does not allow unauthorized copying of content (Marriott 2003). Sony is also converging different technologies with its PSX box, which combines a DVD player and recorder, a digital music player, a television tuner, and a personal video recorder into one unit. The estimated cost for this item will run roughly $400 (Pham and Huffstutter 2003). Some of the converged media will only function with specific brands or music labels. For example, one of the labels owned by BMG, Arista, will not allow its DVD singles to be played in other CD players, but will allow them to be played in Sony's PlayStation 2 machines (Marriott 2003). Sony Music Group merged with BMG a few years ago.

Other Big 4 companies are involved in music and content creation for the games. In the beginning of video game and music synergy, Sony cross-promoted Twisted Sister, Run-D.M.C., and Ozzy Osbourne through its PlayStation 2 Grand Theft game. However, most of the music was previously released. Now, numerous video games feature exclusive material and CD releases now include exclusive music only accessible through video game consoles. For example, the first one million copies of P.O.D.'s Atlantic album "Payable on Death" included an exclusive Sony PlayStation 2 DVD featuring an exclusive non-album track called "Space" (Traiman 2003b). In addition, video game "NFL Street" also featured eleven exclusive unreleased tracks from the Sony label that only play in Sony's PlayStation 2, as well as the Xbox and Nintendo GameCube consoles. Two of the tracks will be made into videos featuring game footage, while other tunes will be sent to radio outlets (Traiman 2004b). In order to hear some of these Sony Label tunes, consumers will again have to buy the hardware, as well as the video games in order to access latest singles and exclusive songs.

Vivendi Universal also works with Sony in the creation and promotion of music-related products. Although they are supposed to be competing as parents of the Big 4 labels, they work together and benefit from each other's promotional campaigns. They also have a joint venture with the online music subscription service Pressplay. Several Vivendi Universal related artists are involved with video games designed for use with Sony Playstation consoles.

Island Def Jam, owned by Vivendi Universal, is also turning to the video game industry to cross-promote products. Vivendi Universal is joining with Electronic Arts, the worlds largest game maker to combine new music releases exclusively in video games (Holloway 2003a). The first game is called "Vendetta" and features twelve Def Jam artists including DMX, Scarface, Method Man, Ghostface Killah, Ludacris, Redman, and others. The new games allow participants to play their favorite musical artist in a wrestling ring while the latest single by each artist plays in the background. The only trick is that the latest singles will not be available in CD format and they won't be played on the radio until after the games have been released for some time.

There are several other examples. Rapper Snoop Dogg's remake of the Doors' tune "Riders in the Storm," which premiered in Need For Speed Underground 2, a video game from Electronic Arts exemplifies this arrangement. It was not on the radio or MTV when it first came out (Robischon 2004). Snoop is a Geffen Records recording artist, which is owned by Vivendi Universal.

Vanessa Carlton, whose parent label is also owned by Vivendi Universal, composed and performed the original theme track "Dark Carnival" for Midway Games' "SpyHunter 2" (Traiman 2004a). Hip-hop artist Black Eyed Peas, whose parent label is also owned by Vivendi Universal provided a soundtrack for "The Urbz: Sims in the City" video game. Some of their vocal tracks were exclusively remixed in "Simlish," the language spoken in the game ("Gaming, Music Industries" 2004). Finally, in the game titled "Area 51," Midway Games announced it would record voiceovers from musician Marilyn Manson (who is also a Vivendi Universal recording artist) in PlayStation 2 during 2005. The video games feature on-screen graphics of the band or musician's name as well as their label. In order to listen to any of the these exclusive tracks through larger and louder speakers, consumers will have to purchase a Sony Computer Playstation Portable device with its Logitech Amp, which sells for roughly $80.

A number of other musicians also share their music or personas with various games such as: Infogames' 'N Sync HotLine Fantasy Phone, Tecmo's Unison (features music by Apollo 440, Naughty by Nature, Nelly, and others) and Konami's Dance Dance Revolution. Sony Computer Entertainment America's Frequency and Uncle Mudfish feature a music video for the new Radica Gamester peripherals line. In addition MTV DJ Funkmaster Flex also plays an onscreen role in Codemasters' MTV Music Generator (Traiman 2001a). Musical artists Barenaked Ladies not only lent one of their singles to the game NHL 2002, but they were also featured in the video game, which came out close to two months before the actual album was released. Metallica, Aerosmith, Blink-182, Papa Roach, and Paul Oakenfold were also featured in video games during 2002 (Traiman 2001c). Finally, Eve lent her voice to a character called "Major

Jones" in a video game entitled "XIII," made by Ubi Soft Entertainment ("Ubi Soft" 2003).

The industry is dividing up exclusive music in video games and releasing them before the music is available for purchase in other formats in hopes of creating multiple sales from one product. The cross-promotion also helps brand recognition. This new form of promotion through media and technology convergence means that fans that do not have one, will have to buy a video game console in order to listen to the single. Indeed, with Vivendi Universal, they are forcing people interested in certain hip-hop artists to purchase additional hardware in order to acquire up-to-date releases. In addition, music fans will be limited to listening to the singles through the video game console. If they like the music enough and want to hear it in their car, home stereo, portable music player or perhaps on a computer, they will have to buy it again, possibly on another multi-song format once it is released.

Here, Vivendi-Universal can make "2 sales" from a musical product that historically was only released on one medium. By creating music in different forms of non-compatible media, Vivendi Universal can bring its profits up in a manner similar to what the introduction of the CD did for sales in the eighties. Again, when this change took place, people purchased the same music on several different formats. They may have purchased the record, 8-track, cassette, and CD of the same music. However, at that time, purchasing a CD player did not force people into doing something else, like play a video game in order to have access to the music.

However, the "2 sales" can work in the opposite direction as well. The video game "Omikron: The Nomad Soul" featured the music and persona of David Bowie through a character named "Boz." The soundtrack was released a month before the actual game for a street price of $40. Here, David Bowie fans may have first purchased the soundtrack, then purchased the video game, which included the soundtrack to see the virtual character portrayed by Bowie. The video game also included an additional "virtual" album characters could purchase and listen to during the game (Traiman 1999b).

Interestingly enough, in the not so distant future video games will direct consumers to more sales of selected products that are imbedded in the actual games. Video games will be "gates" which direct consumers to other entertainment products connected to, or owned by the parent companies. An easy metaphor would parallel this development as a digital vending machine. Here, consoles will become more connected to the Internet, so players will start out simply playing a game, which may be titled after a movie, only to find themselves with several online options for more exclusive content or additional digital products for purchase.

SUPER AUDIO CDS (SACDS) AND AUDIO DVD SINGLES

Besides creating new hardware and media (like video games) for fans to generate additional revenue, the music industry is also creating newer media in hopes of repeating its successful "2 sale" period throughout the eighties and nineties with the transition from vinyl and cassette to compact disc. It is important to remember CDs are cheaper to manufacture than vinyl and the industry re-released back catalogs on the new format, which caused consumers to purchase their favorite albums not once, but twice.

Given that sales of hardcopy music are down and the "2 sales" phenomenon worked so well, the industry is desperately looking for new media to bring its revenue back to the same annual percentage growth it enjoyed from 1980–2000. While it has continued this phenomenon with "remastered" CDs and re-releases with additional tracks, it has also invented two new media, each marketed to a different demographic. One such medium is called a DVD single, which entails surround sound audio with video imagery targeting younger people with youth-oriented pop artists. The next invention is a Super Audio Compact Disc, or SACD, which focuses on an older demographic with more disposable income. As of mid 2004, there were more than 700 DVD-Audio and 2,000 Super Audio CD's available for sale (Walsh 2004).

Each medium contains several audio tracks requiring expensive new hardware for the audio to work correctly. With these new media, the industry hopes to reach four goals: 1) To make money off of SACDS and audio DVDs, 2) To profit from new audio hardware required to play them, 3) To have the new media become accepted by consumers so they repurchase their favorite albums on the new media ("2 sales" phenomenon) and 4) make it more difficult to make copies or to upload and download these media over the Internet.

Indeed, SACDs and DVD singles are more complex than traditional stereo media. Almost every music fan listens to cassettes, records or regular CDs that feature a traditional stereo mix of music featuring unique sounds in speaker A and different sounds in speaker B. This is how music has been created and purchased for decades. SACDs differ because instead of having two stereo outputs, meaning speaker A and speaker B, SACDs enable six speakers to produce unique mixes. Therefore, if a listener has a compatible sound system, she can hear music with distinctly mixed instruments in speakers A-F, similar to a surround sound movie experience. Ultimately SACDs are supposed to conjure the audio experience equated with viewing a movie in a surround sound theater in addition to recreating the frequency response of analog sound. One of the few styles of music where this six-channel music process could work well would be with dub reggae.

Records are considered analog media because they are not made of the zeros and ones that comprise digital media. Music on vinyl is often the preferred mode for deejays because bass frequencies are often deeper and richer than with a digital format. However, CDs have better high-end frequencies because of the limitations of the vinyl production process. When one creates a record, one needs to trim the upper frequencies on the music, otherwise there is a risk of damaging production equipment.

The industry is hoping older, more affluent music fans will now repurchase their favorite albums on their new SACD audio format. Most of the re-releases are classic albums such as Elvis or The Rolling Stones that appeal to this demographic. In fact, what may happen is that fans of these bands may have purchased the album four times if they end up buying SACDs. They may have purchased the initial vinyl release in the seventies, the cassette tape or 8-track tape for their car in the mid-seventies, the standard CD in the eighties or nineties and finally purchased the SACD in the twenty-first century.

Nonetheless, there are limitations to SACDs. Not all SACDs play in regular CD players. "Single Layer" manufactured SACDs may not play on typical CD players. "Hybrid" SACDs will play on a standard CD player, as well as in a SACD player, but the "super audio" feature will only be heard if one has a SACD player with the additional high-priced hardware to make it work. Finally, consumers are limited to sitting in one place, without moving, to hear the so-called "sweet" spot, where all of the sound effects equally come together as one composition.

AUDIO DVDs

Audio DVDs, created by Panasonic, Toshiba and other patent holders, have also recently surfaced on the market place. DVD audio is a "music-centered variation on the standard DVD, usually containing a high-resolution multi-channel mix of the album and additional content like lyrics, photos, band interviews and music videos" (Rothman 2003). Where as SACDs were meant to target older people, the music created on these DVD singles is geared toward younger consumers.

DVD singles on Epic Records feature an average of two videos as well as extra random footage. These DVD singles are being tried as a means of boosting sales. It is hoped that the singles, which sell at list prices from $7.98 to $9.99 will make up for the decline of CD single sales. One explanation for the fall in sales of CD singles comes from the lack of industry support given to digital singles compared with that given to vinyl 45s. During the last two decades the industry had been promoting full length CDs instead of CD singles (Nelson 2003).

DVD singles are similar to SACDs because one must also purchase additional hardware in order for DVD audio disks to work. First, one needs to buy a DVD player with an additional chipset and six outputs for surround sound, or a specifically designed "home theater in a box" system (Rothman 2003). One also needs to buy additional speakers for the surround sound to function. Another option is to purchase a universal player, which can read both DVD and SACD formats. In 2003 they ran for over $500, but were expected to lower in the following years. One still needs to purchase the additional "satellite" speakers, a subwoofer and a center channel (Rothman 2003). High-end automobile manufacturers such as Cadillac, Mercedes-Benz, and Volvo are also designing cars with these audio capabilities. Interested consumers will need to spend over $3,000 for the audio equipment not including installation.

Similar to SACDs, industry executives are hoping DVD singles will slow down consumer interest in downloading songs for free from the Internet. DVD copying and uploading on the Internet is more difficult and less frequent than music downloading. In this respect, the music industry appears to be using DVD singles as another weapon against free music downloading. Because youth are more likely to upload and download music on the Internet, targeting them with audio DVDs makes "good" business sense.

Nonetheless, DVD-audio disks have a number of limitations. First, in order for them to work appropriately, they cannot be listened to in portable players. Therefore, listeners wanting to see and hear new material will be limited to the confines of their home "studios," or one of a few types of high-end automobiles. Second, DVD-Audio discs are not compatible with regular CD players and some DVD singles such as Arista DVD singles will not play in CD players, but will play in some video game consoles (Marriott 2003). They also force consumers to be in one place in order to hear all of the different music tracks as they were meant to be heard.

CONCLUSION

While DVD singles have limitations concerning portability, what SACDs, video games and various audio hardware have in common, is that while these technologies are converging, they also appear to limit access to information and culture based on owners' financial capabilities. Ultimately, if one is interested in listening to new songs by artists on different labels, one may have to purchase a video game, console, television, DVD player, surround sound stereo system, subscribe to an Internet Service Provider, or rent the song through an online distribution site instead of merely listening to it on the radio or going to the store to purchase a single. Consumers are spending more money to listen to music now than ever before.

In addition, this chapter supports McCourt and Burkart (2003) and Freedman's (2003) argument that music companies are using technology to protect their positions via copyright restrictions on copying through the creation of new media where uploading content is more difficult. However, the music industry is also doing this not only by anti-copying software technologies or new media, but also by creating "keys and locks" in various hardware components. Here, consumers have music locked in various hardware or media, but need to spend additional money to access the music either through additional hardware or subscription services (keys).

This chapter also examined the connections between the Big 4 and various electronics and computer manufacturers. It traced the ownership of CD burners, MP3 players and video games, while noting which ones were owned by music industry parent companies. These new technologies are creating exclusive musical content through separate media. Finally, this chapter also investigated new media the music industry is hoping will replace standard CDs in hopes of gaining addition sales, through the creation of a new media replacement cycle. The argument presented suggests the conglomerate structured music industry's business plan is to spark multiple sales through new hardware and media forms with exclusive music.

CHAPTER 6

FILE SHARING AND INDUSTRY SALES

This chapter traces influences that created value for the Big 4 during 1999 to 2004, which was a period where the music industry argued it incurred incredible financial loses resulting from file sharing through services such as Napster and Kazaa. Because each music division exists within a conglomerate that makes a number of different products and services linked to their music divisions, accurate estimates of exact value are quite difficult. In fact, very few people know how much money the industry gains or loses. Only a small number of people have access to these figures and they can't discuss them because of confidentiality policies (Bulter 2005b).

While Chapters 4 and 5 examined the revenue conglomerates earn through royalties and sales of electronic hardware, this chapter focuses on additional production-oriented mechanisms that influence the economic well-being of the music industry. It examines how artist rosters, the elimination of CD singles and the economy affect industry value. It also describes how new media sales, increases in artist, marketing and production costs, employee lay-offs, the end of the CD-replacement cycle, changing demographics and used CD sales influence profits for the Big 4. This chapter argues the net result of sales decreases during 2000–2004 did not mean the music industry was losing massive amounts of money, nor did it mean it was going bankrupt or "out of business." Several of the Big 4 companies appear to have maintained profitability during this time frame, which suggests file sharing has been having a minimal impact on industry net worth and that the music industry will be around for some time to come.

Nonetheless, one does not have to look far to find the argument that the music industry is about to collapse. Entire issues of contemporary magazines such as Wired have been devoted to this topic. Most articles suggest the industry is losing massive amounts of money due to file sharing services, which allow people to swap music for free. The industry argues the invention of file sharing services like Napster, Morpheus, Gnutella, Kazaa, Grokster, and eDonkey have seriously damaged the music industry and as a result, the public should feel culpable for driving the labels into such a negative financial predicament. In fact, the public is taught to believe the music industry is in such dire straights that perhaps its time to start community bake sales at senior centers across the country to raise money for their survival. The industry continues to argue people who ordinarily purchased music were now buying less because they could get it for free. In fact, Mercer Management Consulting VP Jon Fay analyzed the retail value of songs downloaded from Napster if they were to be sold as albums and concluded the value would be $30 to $40 billion (Garrity 2001b). Therefore, the music industry was losing billions of dollars from online file sharing, correct?

Yet for some "strange" reason, the music industry was not losing billions of dollars from file trading during this period, even though on the surface the argument against file sharing services appears valid. There has been a two-year decline in cassette and compact disc sales from retail stores, which has harmed retailers (Holson 2003c). According to Nielsen SoundScan, which tracks album sales, 681 million albums were sold in 2002, down from 785 million in 2000. The decline in sales has paralleled the invention of file sharing services. However, the argument that hardcopy sales losses can be solely attributed to the invention of file sharing services is highly flawed.

What is missing in this equation is that total sales of albums continued to rise during Napster's short lifespan (Alderman 2001). Album sales increased by 5.9 percent from 1998–1999 and by 4 percent from 1999–2000 (Christman 2001a). At the same time, record club sales were not counted by Soundscan and some direct-TV music sales were not counted either, which suggests these are conservative estimates (Garrity 2005a). U.S sales increased as well, even though the U.S. had the highest number of users downloading music from Napster according to a Jupiter Media Metrix study. It had 13.6 million users in February 2001, even though Canada had the highest percentage of at-home users in the world with 30.3 percent, followed by Argentina with 25 percent, Spain with 23.8 percent, Brazil with 18.8 percent, and the United States with 16.1 percent (Garrity 2001c). Album sales began to decline only after Napster's demise.

The irony with the music industry's policy and war against file sharing services is that the industry also uses them to its own gain. Most of the major labels hire firms to track peer-to-peer downloading for trends and for gauging what kinds of tracks and genres appear popular (Banerjee 2004a). These peer-to-peer services are good testing grounds for the music industry because they help them decide which artists or genres to throw advertising dollars behind. Sometimes the labels can even see who is searching for what tunes based on zip code. Ultimately the kind of information obtained from peer-to-peer sites is extremely valuable for the Big 4. They can monitor the activity, then call radio stations to push the artists that are popular from this information, as well as determine which artists to push with more advertising dollars.

Putting aside the music industry's obvious hypocrisy with trying to shut down something it also prospers from, it is curious this information is not more present in the news media given the decline in music industry hardcopy sales was such a hot news topic. Apparently only the information that would benefit the industry dominated the media, while the potentially damaging information was sidelined.

SHIPMENTS, VALUE AND MUSIC INDUSTRY STOCK: 1999–2004

As noted in the preceding section, global hardcopy format sales began decreasing around 2000 and continued to decrease through at least 2003. Nonetheless, just because sales were decreasing in certain formats, did not mean the Big 4 were losing massive amounts of money directly as a result of file sharing. Moreover, because profitability involves a number of different factors such as businesses plans, artist rosters, market shares, investments, marketing costs, internal economic dynamics, as well as others influences, sales are not the only indicator of value. The irony behind all of their complaints is that the industry continues to be profitable during its transition into digital and wireless distribution. Here is a brief history of industry value indicating some of the different influences affecting overall performance starting in 1999.

Dollar-value of worldwide music sales in 1999 grew by 1.5 percent, while the U.S market grew by eight percent ("World Soundcarrier" 2000). It is important to note market values often change depending on what currency is used as a determinant. For example, during the same time period, the value of the Japanese music market fell 6 percent in yen terms, but rose 20 percent in dollar terms ("1999 World" 2000). Discrepancies in value are frequent, which result from currency fluctuations. Valuing markets using constant dollars, which provides a better sense of revenue for the Big 4, minimizes the impact of currency fluctuations. Constant dollar rates consist of the average rates of the U.S. dollar per year as published by the International Monetary Fund.

In 2000, the retail value of global music sales decreased by two percent, while the U.S. market grew by 4 percent in unit terms according to SoundScan ("US slowdown" 2001). Album sales in chain stores increased by 1.6 percent to 430.4 million units over 1999. Mass merchants also increased by 4.9 percent, independent retailers by 6.4 percent and nontraditional retailers went up by 55.6 percent (Christman 2001a).

The 2001 music market also declined. Global CD album shipments fell by 125 million units from 2000. Global recorded music shipments fell in retail value by 4.5 percent to $33.7 billion from $35.3 billion the year before (Masson 2002). One of the reasons for the decline in sales was the phasing out of CD singles and cassettes. Total shipments of these media in 1998 accounted for roughly 250 million units valued close to two billion dollars (a $1.42 billion dollar value for cassette albums, $213 million for CD singles and $94.4 million for cassette singles) (Jeffrey 1999). The industry lost a lot of money phasing out these media, even though consumer demand still existed.

Music sales continued to decline during the first five months of 2001 partially because there was a lack of blockbuster new releases during this period. During the first five months of 2000, the industry saw major releases by 'N Sync, Britney Spears, and Eminem, which all sold close to ten million copies each during this time frame (Benz 2001a). In 2001, blockbuster releases such as Linkin Park, Shaggy, Enya, and 'N Sync sold far fewer units as compared to the artists of the previous year. The U.S economy was also sluggish during 2001, leading it into a recession. The aftermath of the September 11th attacks did not improve sales and the economy continued to decline, while shopping and general consumption also went down. According to one retailer, "Music sales are not terrible. They're just not great" (Garrity 2001e). Consumers avoided mall shopping and practiced more discretionary spending. Finally, touring by musical artists was also curtailed, which meant a decrease in revenue from concert and merchandise sales.

Even while sales were dropping during the end of 2001, some Big 4 companies were still able to increase cash flow over the same time period from the previous year. For example, UMG, despite a sales decline of 4 percent during the third quarter of 2001, saw its earnings rise to $227 million from $213 million in the same period last year (Benz 2001c).

Going into 2002, total album sales continued to decline. Global music sales declined by 7.6 percent from 2001 to 2002, which was driven by a 6 percent drop in CD album sales, a 16 percent drop in single sales and a 36 percent drop in cassette sales. These figures do not include music video unit sales (Masson 2003). Nonetheless, even while global sales declined, WMG maintained its profitability during 2002, while BMG returned to profitability during the same period (Hardy 2003g). The increase in profitability resulted from several restructuring initiatives such as the trimming of artist rosters and the downsizing of employees.

Restructuring also earned additional profits for at least three of the Big 4 music companies during the first six months of 2003. Sales at WMG rose 2 percent during this time frame and enjoyed an 8 percent increase in revenues as well (Hardy 2003f). EMI also increased its total number of albums sold from 27.4 million to 28.6 million during this period (Hardy 2003e). However, UMG's revenues in the first six months of 2003 fell 35 percent (15 percent in constant currency terms) to $2,431 million. UMG blamed the losses on adverse currency movements and the continued weakness of the global soundcarrier market

(Hardy 2003c). For Sony, (SMEI) sales in the U.S. fell by 8 percent, while SMEJ (Sony's Japanese music division) rose by 11 percent to $263 million (Hardy 2003d). Japan is the world's second largest music market.

Even while global music sales fell 7.6 percent in 2003 to $32 billion ("'Music Slump" 2004), the actual stock of many U.K. and U.S. music-related media, retail and technology companies rose during the same timeframe. In fact, there were double-digit percentage gains over the 2002 closing stock prices (Garrity and Brandle 2004). For example, Vivendi Universal, parent of Universal Music Group closed 2003 with its stock up 51 percent while shares in Time Warner were up 37 percent from the previous year. Nonetheless, Sony posted a 16 percent decline, while EMI's stock lost value, except for its shares in music pureplay, which went up 15 percent at the end of 2003 (Garrity and Brandle 2004). Even though the previous shake-out and dot.com bubble caused the loss of several hundred million dollars, online sales continued to increase by 8.4 percent from 2002 to 2003 according to Nielsen SoundScan, although it is not clear if this figure refers to hardcopy sales or digital sales online (Koehn 2003). Nonetheless, increasing sales from downloads and revenue from subscription services may have affected stock values. It is likely that they were not counted previous to 2004 because Neilson SoundScan was not counting digital album sales or revenue from subscription services (Garrity 2004a).

What is interesting is that there is often a minimal relationship between sales, profitability and market shares. For example, during 2002, UMG increased its market share, but its sales and profitability fell. At the same time, EMI's operating profits rose by 33 percent despite an 11 percent sales decrease. BMG also experienced lower sales but enjoyed higher operating profits, while WMG saw both its profits and sales rise with an increase in market share. EMI, which experienced a drop in global market share, experienced the highest profit margin of all the Big 4 during this time. Ultimately EMI, BMG, and WMG all experienced higher profits in 2002 mostly due to their cost-cutting exercises from the previous year (Hardy 2003a).

Moving on into 2004, the International Federation of the Phonographic Industry noted that world shipments of physical formats in 2004 was valued at $33.6 billion, which was a decline of 1.3 percent from 2003 (Legrand 2005). CD album shipments, which accounted for 86 percent of the total shipments, were valued at $28.9 billion, which were down .9 percent from 2003 (Legrand 2005). However, sales in 2004 increased dramatically over the previous years. U.S. album sales were up for the first time in four years according to Ed Christman (2005) of Billboard Magazine. Total sales, which now started to include digital sales as well, increased by close to 20 percent during this same period to 817 million units. In 2003, a total of 687 million units were sold. In 2004, digital track sales came in at over 141 million, while digital albums reached 5.5 million (Christman 2005). A report by the International Federation of Phonographic Industry (IFPI) put online worldwide sales for 2004 at $300 million and expected the sales to double for 2005 (Koranteng 2005a). Another estimate put download sales at 1-1.5 percent of overall market value, which for 2004 would have meant $336-490 million (Legrand 2005). Around this time, EMI Group Chairman Eric Nicoli projected "Digital growth will far outstrip physical decline over the next five years" (Brandle 2005). The numbers were starting to suggest he was correct. Weekly digital track sales went from a little over 200,000 in July of 2003, to more than 2.4 million a year later (Garrity 2004d).

In addition to hard copy and digital sales, music video increased 26.3 percent to $2.7 billion, which was mostly due to the popularity of music DVDs (Walsh 2005). Music DVD shipments were up by 23.2 percent, which valued them at $2.7 billion in 2004. This format constituted 8 percent of the total market in 2004, versus just 6 percent in 2003 (Legrand 2005). In terms of stock value, EMI Group saw its stock jump 53 percent, Sony went up 9.7 percent and Vivendi Universal by 15 percent while Time Warner fell 2.28 percent after selling WMG the first six months of 2004 (Garrity 2004c).

ADDITIONAL MECHANISMS AFFECTING VALUE

While the economy, the September 11th attacks, and the decline of the CD single affected the value of the music industry, additional influences impacted the market as well. Convergence of music-related technology, the phasing out of different media, increasing marketing and production costs, as well as corporate lay-offs influenced overall value. Because music is now released in video games, through DVDs, or online, excluding high DVD sales or video game sales from music divisions can make a financial situation look worse that it may be. In addition, highly profitable DVD sales included in music division financial results can often mask loses of CD sales for an artist. At a time when sales of compact discs have dropped and music DVDs are increasing, total DVD sales have been skyrocketing.

Besides the convergence of music-related media, different recorded media also affect the total number of sales for the industry. It is important to know that media corporations phase out certain media in favor of newer or better selling formats. That is why records and Beta video tapes are harder to find and VHS tapes will eventually disappear in favor of DVDs. The music industry began doing this by phasing out less expensive products like CD singles and cassettes at roughly the same time it began complaining about sales losses from Napster ("Why Experts" 2003). When they were still being manufactured, SoundScan counted CD singles and cassettes. However when these products became less available, although not as a result of consumer demand, SoundScan registered an obvious decrease in the total number of music sales. Ironically, the music industry phased out singles in hopes of forcing consumers to purchase albums so more profit could be made. Now the industry also wants to force people into the online and wireless world to purchase digital singles where more profit is made over hardcopy single CDs or records. For example, it can cost $4,500-5,000 to manufacture and mail a small run of CD singles specifically for radio (Stark 2004). With digital singles, there are no production or mailing costs, so emailing new releases in a digital format to stations saves the music industry money. Forcing consumers to purchase digital singles also saves the industry money.

The merging of companies and bad accounting create additional consequences that affect the music industry's total value. Although AOL Time Warner enjoyed $480 million in operating profits in 2002, it was still $29 billion in debt, most of which was generated from its decision to merge AOL and Time Warner (Kirkpatrick 2003a). Vivendi Universal lost more than $25 billion in 2002 largely as a result of huge write-offs on investments made during the bubble booming 1990's (Tagliabue 2003).

Increasing artist costs, as well as fees for marketing and production also affect the financial standing of the music industry. Sony's music division lost more than $132 million in 2002, but largely because of higher artist costs (Holson and Holloway 2003). As a means of adjusting and compensating for sales losses, the music industry has been creating shorter and sometimes less expensive contracts with major artists (Holson and Fabrikant 2003). It is also spending less because the costs of marketing, recording, talent acquisition and development also have increased (Benz, Christman, and Garrity 2003). For example, Universal Music Group experienced an operating income drop of 89 percent in the third quarter of 2002, largely from marketing and development costs, although it expected a substantial increase in sales after holiday profits were calculated in with the fourth quarter (Holson and Fabrikant 2003). In addition, from 2001–2003 WMG lost $8 billion, but 90 percent of their loses came from Time Warner-related write-downs, meaning it lost billions from a pre-tax asset impairment charge, a non-cash charge resulting from a sales accounting charge and other charges. (Christman 2004c).

While costs have ultimately increased, the industry has also saved money with employee lay-offs (Holson 2003c). For example, BMG Entertainment's employee roster shrunk by 2,806 employees from 1999 to 2001 ("BMG Entertainment" 2003), while Sony Music Entertainment laid off 500 employees in 2000 ("Sony Music" 2003). In addition, EMI laid off 20 percent of its workforce in 2001 ("EMI Group" 2003). It also announced it would lay-off 1,500 jobs, or about another 19 percent of its staff in April of 2004 ("'Music Slump'" 2004). Time Warner also laid off around a quarter of it's employees in France as well (Clark 2004). In October of 2003, Universal Music Group announced it would cut 800 jobs ("Race To Merge" 2003), while the more recent Sony-BMG merger was to result in 2000 lay-offs in an effort to cut over $300 million in operational costs (Conniff 2004). Sony was also expected to cut several thousand more positions worldwide through 2006 (McClure 2003).

END OF THE CD-REPLACEMENT CYCLE?

While mergers, higher artist costs and marketing expenses may have affected the value of the music industry, the end of the CD-replacement cycle may have done the most harm to sales. It is important to remember the invention of the compact disc was premised on the assumption that baby boomers would be likely to replace their vinyl collection with CDs. This industry assumption proved quite profitable throughout the eighties and nineties. However, what the music industry did not plan for was the long-term course of action once the majority of baby boomers had replaced their collections on a CD format. What has happened is that this cycle may have now run its course, with most baby boomers already having repurchased their original albums on disc. Industry analysts like Terri Santisi, the global leader of the media and entertainment group at KPMG, agree. Terri noted the industry was not in turmoil, but that it was in transition because the CD replacement cycle, which had driven the majority of profits over the last twenty years had run its course (Benz, Christman, and Garrity 2003).

Newer transitional formats include SACDS, Audio DVDs, and digital downloads from the Internet and wireless carriers. The problem for the music industry is to continually create new musical formats that will replace older ones in order to sustain high profits. They can either do this by changing the technology in which the formats are played, or by changing the media themselves every few years. Presently, the industry is doing both. As long as the industry continually changes either one or both of these two important components in their business plan, and the public responds semi-favorably to it, then it will continue to reap in profits for decades to come. For the public, this means it will have to continue purchasing new technology in order to play new releases, subscribe to more "pay-per-access" services in order to listen to music, as well as purchase the same music over and over time again.

The CD replacement cycle has also evolved into a re-issue cycle by re-releasing older bands in new "greatest hits" or re-mastered formats. Sales of these "deep-catalog" albums, defined by the industry as products in release for more than three years dropped by 11 percent in 2002, declining more than twice as much as sales from new releases. These "deep-catalog" releases represent 25 percent of the industry's sales accounting for roughly 177 million albums sold (Leeds 2003). Sales of these older albums have been supporting the industry and provide huge profits because they cost relatively nothing to promote given they already have brand awareness and huge followings. Breaking in new artists can be costly and risky given that audience reactions are not always certain. Because sales of these catalog items are beginning to decrease, one could suggest most consumers are already familiar with the artists, and that younger people may not be interested in another re-release of Twisted Sister, Barbara Streisand, Yanni, or Bob Segar and the Silver Bullet Band's "Greatest Hits" CD. In fact, the timeline for these bands may be coming to an end because of changes in demographics and music tastes.

Labels also make additional revenue from artists by releasing several versions of the same material. This includes both hardcopy and digital sales. Here, consumers purchase several of the same songs more than once. They may purchase different versions of the same CD with each version including one or two exclusive tracks. For example, Warner Brothers recently released three different versions of Josh Gorban's "Closer" CD. The initial release, dated November 11th, 2003 included thirteen tracks and sold for roughly $14.00. A limited edition CD/DVD of the same music plus two more tracks for roughly $28.00 also came out. For fans still interested in more, they had to wait almost six months later to purchase the "Fan Edition," which featured all of the same tracks, the DVD, plus two more tracks than the limited edition CD/DVD. The later "Fan Edition" sold for over $30 when it first came out on the market. Given the timing of these releases, one could assume thousands of fans purchased the same music twice and possible three times in order to hear the additional tracks, which were released several months later. Eileen Meehan (2005) refers to a similar process in the television and film industries as "reversioning." Here companies make additional revenues from products by releasing second versions that offer more material.

Ultimately, the industry failed to factor in the end of the CD replacement cycle and did not prepare as well as it should have in advance for this shift. At the same time, predicting the uses of new technology is difficult. It was fortunate to have enjoyed massive profits during the last two decades, in part due to this technological shift and its ability to convince consumers they would need to upgrade their music collections by repurchasing the same music on a different format — the "2 sales" phenomenon. As chapter 5 already suggested, the industry is hoping it will be able to create another replacement cycle with the recent invention of SACDS and audio DVDs. Even though these cycles are becoming more well known, the press prefer to reiterate the industry's stance, which argues file swapping is the *raison d'etre* for recent sales declines.

CHANGING DEMOGRAPHICS, PRICING AND USED CDS ALSO BEHIND SALES DECLINES?

Besides sales declines of hardcopy CDs from the CD replacement cycle, National Association of Recording Merchandisers (NARM) Chairman Peter Cline noted in a recent speech that the blockbuster music product coming out of the major labels does not appear to reflect the growing diversity of the consumer base in the United States. He indicated that Latin and African-Americans constitute more than 25 percent of the population and that the average age of the population is increasing. As a result, certain mass appeal music groups may not be received as well by all groups within society, which may eventually drain blockbuster sales and lead to a more segmented music market (Garrity and Christman 2002).

It is also possible baby boomers may have decided to discontinue purchasing reissues and new music due to prohibitive costs. Consumers may have viewed the $18.98 CD retail price as simply too expensive. Instead of going down between the eighties and the nineties, CD prices actually increased until a recent price-fixing investigation exposed the music industry of over-charging for its product. In June of 2003, a judge approved a settlement in a music antitrust lawsuit that was supposed to result in more than 3.5 million consumers receiving checks of roughly $13.00 each ("Judge: Millions" 2003). This ruling suggested distributors and retailers conspired to inflate CD prices, which resulted in a retail price reduction for commercial compact discs. According to the FTC, price fixing in the U.S. had cost consumers $480 million dollars from 1997 through the end of 2000 ("Tracking" 2001). Although a check for a mere $13 may be little compared to profits the industry made from the hundreds of CDs some consumers purchased during the last twenty years, it does demonstrate that the courts have not entirely been co-opted by corporate America. At the same time, I registered for my $13 several years ago and have yet to receive the check.

Compact disc pricing has been an interesting phenomenon to observe because it not only changes due to legal decisions, but also due to consumer demand. It is now a well-known secret that music labels increase prices once artists become popular. These "New Artist Prices," that the distributors set for selling to retailers, are lower than the prices they set for more established artists. But retail stores, not the distribution companies or the labels, ultimately set prices. They decide on how much profit they want to make from the product. For example, new artist CDs are often sold to stores for around six to seven dollars per CD. The store may then decide to sell the CD for ten to thirteen dollars. However, when sales begin to increase, like the case of Macy Gray, then the distribution companies significantly boost the price of the CD sometimes by over a 100 percent. Instead of selling the CD wholesale to stores for six to seven dollars, suddenly the price has increased to eleven to thirteen dollars. After people began to purchase Macy Gray's CD, the label nearly doubled the prices to the distributors and retail stores, responding to the increase in demand.[1]

Pricing can also work in the opposite direction. Stores such as Best Buy may set prices extremely low on certain CDs in order to advertise itself as "The Store" to buy them. The goal is to undercut the competition by luring consumers into the store with a few under-priced, popular CDs, in hopes that they purchase more expensive electronic hardware where higher profit margins are made. In fact, most stores do not make incredible amounts of money from compact disc sales.

Finally, the proliferation of DVDs and video games may make consumers believe they can get more for less when they buy media other than CDs. Instead of buying just music, consumers get music and image through DVDs for the same and sometimes lower price as a CD. In fact, high costs appear to be fueling the massive pirated CD market outside of the United States. Some figures suggest that two out of every five CDs are now pirated ("Pirate CD" 2003). However, in countries where the average wage is still $150 a month and large percentages of households live below the poverty line, the music industry has little hope of selling CDs for $15 when a pirated CD can be the equivalent of 4 dollars. To illustrate the changes between economies more clearly, a person making $2000 a month in the United States would end up spending $200 per CD within this pricing scenario.

Other people may still be buying just as many CDs as before, but have now decided to purchase more used CDs instead of new ones, possibly due to prohibitive costs. There has indeed been a growth in used CD sales during the past few years. For example, Amazon.com's third party sales of used musical product increased from 2 percent in 2001 to 12 percent in 2002 when comparing the first quarter of each year. Amazon, Ebay, and Half.com have all been able to increase business by offering used music sales. So have traditional retail stores. According to David Lang, president of CD World, a ten store chain in New Jersey, "In December [of 2001], our used CD business was up 80 percent over last year" (Garrity, Benz, and Christman 2002). Other retailers have also been trying to get into the action as well. Trans World retailers recently acquired online used-CD business secondspin.com, while Tower is also expanding its used CD sections. Unfortunately the number of used CD sales does not register with SoundScan, so exact numbers are difficult to compare with recent sales decreases in new albums.

Even though used sales would appear helpful to the Big 4 in terms of sparking consumer interest in new music, the industry is against the selling of used CDs. So far, music industry attempts to clamp down on used CD sales have been mostly unsuccessful due to "first sales" rules in the Copyright Act, which allow for the resale of goods after their purchase. However these laws do not apply to sales of digital music downloads. Therefore, by moving consumers online where they can buy digital downloads, the music industry can expand its profit base and circumvent the "first sales" component of the Copyright Act.

CONCLUSION

This chapter cited evidence against the argument that file sharing is the main cause behind decreased sales for the music industry. It argued production-oriented mechanisms such as the trimming of artist rosters, the elimination of CD singles and employee lay-offs influenced the value of the industry during 1999 to 2004. In addition, the economic recession, the attacks of September 11th, increases in artist, marketing and production costs, the end of the CD-replacement cycle, changing demographics and used CD sales also continue to influence profitability for the Big 4. Even though global sales of hardcopy formats decreased during 2000–2003, several Big 4 companies appear to have maintained profitability during this period, which suggests file sharing technology had a minimal impact on industry net worth. Furthermore, it does not appear to have empowered independent musicians to such an extent they were able to influence the collapse of the industry. In fact, the music industry is here to stay for some time to come.

NOTES

1. Interview with Daniel Sigelman, former music distributor in Minneapolis, Minnesota, August, 2002.

CHAPTER 7

TOWARDS A "SECURE" DIGITAL FUTURE

"We have the right to control the property we own the way we want to"
—David Munns, Chief Executive of EMI North
America (Harmon 2003e)

While the previous chapter introduced and examined various influences affecting the value of the music industry, this chapter focuses on the music industry's response to challenges in copyright infringement, which it claims is driving recent sales loses. It begins by examining the notion of "fair use" and how it is related to the debate on file sharing and CD copying. The second part describes the music industry's success in influencing the legal system through its political lobby group, which has been able to write laws, as well as manipulate various political platforms in its favor. The third section describes how laws have enabled the creation of different forms of digital rights management technologies, as well as how they work. Because the public's reception to these new laws and technologies has not been warm, the music industry has transformed itself into a pseudo policing organization in its pursuit of counter fitters and file traders. Finally, although these industry pursuits would assume large numbers of people are downloading music and that sales are down, recent surveys are suggesting this may not be the case. Therefore, because the industry started developing digital rights management technology at a time when music sales were at an all time high, this chapter argues the music industry is using its wealth and political influence to manipulate the legal system in its favor, while using fear of arrest as a means of forcing people into subscribing to "legitimate," or Big 4 supported music services, where more profit can be made compared to traditional hardcopy sales. The result of these industry tactics question not only constitutionally protected notions of "fair use," but also the public's ability to operate free from government and private interests in the online world.

QUESTION OF FAIR USE

What is at the heart of both digital and non-digital debates on copyright is the notion of fair use. Fair use is a limited freedom based in the Constitution to quote or in the case of music, copy. Fair use evolved during the nineteenth and twentieth centuries to eventually become codified in the Copyright Act of 1976. This law allows users to make copies of, quote from, or refer to copyrighted works for the following purposes: in the course of news reporting; in connection with criticism or comment on the work; for teaching or classroom use; or as part of scholarship or research (Vaidhyanathan 2001).

Courts must decide if an individual has violated fair use given the following criteria: the purpose or character of the use, meaning if it was meant for commercial or educational use; the nature of the original, copyrighted work; the amount of the copyrighted work that was taken or used in the subsequent work; and the effect on the market value of the original work. Concerning music, "courts have ruled that consumers are allowed to make copies of compact discs for use in their own tape players, and may record television broadcasts for later home viewing, as long as they do not sell the copies or display them in a public setting that might dilute the market value of the original broadcast" (Vaidhyanathan 2001). However, Section 1201(a) of the Digital Millennium Copyright Act (DMCA) makes it illegal in the U.S. to circumvent password and encryption systems in order to access, use or copy certain media works, even for fair use purposes (Hardy 2000d).

According to Mann (2000), most legal scholars propose that the writers of the Constitution viewed copyright and fair use in utilitarian terms. The Founders hoped to stimulate the creation of new ideas by allowing a temporary monopoly on their distribution, whereby the creator of the idea was rewarded for a limited time period while the idea passed on to the commons, where people could do what they wanted to with it. However, the music industry's current campaign is pushing for regulation over the distribution of culture, which is inconsistent with the conception of the commons that lies at the root of democracy. The creation of new technology that disables consumers with the ability to make copies during any given time period appears to question this constitutional concept.

In general, the music and movie industries combined with some software and computer manufacturers are not supportive of ensuring that the public has the right to make an additional copy of copyrighted material for non-commercial purposes. The Business Software Alliance and the Computer Systems Policy Project were not supportive of legislation in the spring of 2003, which would have bolstered the rights of people to use copyrighted material digitally (Harmon 2003a). The legislation introduced by Virginia Democrat Rick Boucher evoked the fair use doctrine for the digital world in an attempt to change the 1998 Digital Millennium Copyright Act. Boucher's goal was to ensure that consumers could make fair use of digital copyrighted material through making additional copies of music or DVDs for home or office use even when the material is secured with various forms of technology meant to prevent "illegal" copying.

Mr. Von Lohmann of the Electronic Frontier Foundation notes that making noncommercial mix CDs or home copies of previously purchased CDs is probably legal under the fair use provision of copyright law, but that the law has not been tested in court yet. Because of the 1992 Audio Home Recording Act, people who copy CDs may be exempt from prosecution because a certain percentage of blank disc prices goes to the music industry (Gallagher 2003).

Nonetheless, the music industry argues it loses money when people download or copy music. As a result, the recording industry's trade association, the Recording Industry Association of America (RIAA) has been watching and policing bootleggers, as well as lobbying the government to enact laws favorable to the industry. The RIAA was established to reflect large commercial interests, not the interests of artists or the public. It also has substantial power and money, which enables it to hire expensive lawyers to defend and promote the music industry's goals. Alderman (2001) notes the RIAA often targets small and underfunded companies that cannot necessarily afford to fight them back. It also spent $1.7 million for "governmental relations projects," $1.3 million in "federal legislative support," and $480,000 in "state legislative support" during 2002. The RIAA also has a political action committee or PAC, which spent $630,000 on federal candidates and another $535,000 in soft money on other politicians in 2002 (Ralis 2003). The RIAA's not-for-profit status by the Internal Revenue Service means it does not have to pay taxes to the government. Its money has entitled the music industry with substantial political influence.

The industry's influence is no more apparent than in the previously mentioned 1998 Digital Millennium Copyright Act, which enabled copyright holders the right to circumvent normal judicial processes in pursuing people who downloaded music files. Normally under the Fourth Amendment of the U.S. Constitution, police must show probable cause that a crime has been committed before they can get a judge's permission to search one's home for evidence, or provide a subpoena to appear in court. With the DMCA, all the RIAA has to do is file paperwork with a court clerk to get a subpoena if it suspects someone of downloading music. The influence is apparent because the industry helped write the law. It also requires Internet Service Providers (ISPs) to give copyright holders information when there is a good-faith reason to believe copyrights are being infringed according to lawyers for the RIAA ("Record labels" 2003).

In general, a "secure digital future," where making copies of music and other digital items is impossible may eventually turn into a reality. Lessig (2001) notes that the Internet's current trajectory may eventually create a system of near perfect copyright control. Industry people appear to agree. According to an industry statement made in May of 2003, Apple, Dell, EMI Recorded Music, BMG, Microsoft, HP, Intel, Universal Music Group, Sony Music Entertainment, and Warner Music Group all "felt that significant progress" has been made concerning copyright protection and that discussions concerning "security" were "extremely positive" ("Joint Statement" 2003).

Besides perfect copyright control, Lessig (2001) also fears a world where corporate surveillance of consumer activity will eventually become a reality. As a result of industry-sponsored meetings, a number of different "security measures" for copyright enforcement have been introduced in various forms, including surveillance, while even more appear in the works. Ultimately, corporations see the new Digital Millennium Copyright Act and its emphasis on copyright protection as an opportunity for growth. According to a spokesperson for Macrovision, a specialist in digital-rights management and CD copy-protection technologies, "Digital-rights management and copy-protection solutions for the worldwide music industry represent one of Macrovision's most important growth opportunities" (Garrity 2002b). In 1997, the U.S. copyright industries contributed and estimated $348.4 billion to the economy making up 4.3 percent of the gross domestic product or GDP. In addition, the average growth of the copyright industries since 1993 has been between an astonishing 10.4-13.3 percent, which is one of the fastest growing rates in the economy (Holland 2000).

NEW TECHNOLOGY TO PREVENT CD COPYING

There are numerous companies working on their own form of "digital rights management" or DRM. A three-way approach is underway aimed at preventing consumers from being able to make copies of music. The first level is aimed at preventing people from being able to make additional copies of hardcopy compact discs. The second level focuses on the Internet by trying to prevent copying, while the third level employs technology, which disables the ability to transfer music to and from various electronics devices. This last level is more hardware-oriented.

The first technology used to prevent consumers from being able to make copies of compact discs is Macrovision's safe audio, which degrades the coding in original music. As a result of the degradation of the quality of the music, CD burners will not be able to read the actual disc because of the encoded errors, which is supposed to prohibit copying of the CD (Pohlmann 2001). Macrovision also has plans to work on additional projects aimed at facilitating controlled CD burning and export of music files to consumer electronic devices.

Sony's Key2audio also tries to prevent CDs from being played on home computers, which would prevent them from being uploaded onto the Internet. Instead of encoding errors in the music, Key2audio masks audio files as data files, which prevents CD burning because the programs can't find any audio tracks and therefore cannot copy them. Sony DADC also announced the release of a new SecuROM encryption signature technology called Metamorphosis. It prevents one-on-one copying based on arranging and rearranging code ("The Next Generation" 2003). Another technology referred to as "second-session" technology, enables the placement of two versions of an album on one CD. One version does not allow for any digital copying in any format, but plays on traditional CD players, while the second enables the CD to be played on a computer. It also enables the album to be copied onto a hard drive, but it does not allow the music to be burned on a blank CD (Garrity 2003a).

In terms of quantity of copyproof discs, EMI has distributed more than 127 million copyprotected discs worldwide since 2001. They have prevented consumers from playing and copying discs on computers. As of 2005, EMI was working on technology which would allow users to make only one copy of an entire CD per computer, burn any individual track seven times and make up to three full copies of each album. Consumers will not be able to make a copy of their copy because the discs will be "sterilized" (Garrity 2005d). Other technologies used to prevent copying are Midbar Tech's Cactus Data Shield and SunnComm's MediaCloq. By the time this book is published, newer technologies will also be incorporated into compact discs, hardware and other formats as well.

While the first level of copyproof technologies focuses primarily on the copying of hardcopy compact discs, the second level of DRM focuses on copyright protection on the Internet. One such technology simply vanishes music files over a brief time period through "expiration dates." Here, online songs and movies expire after a single play unless consumers pay the copyright holder ("Self-Destruct Files" 2003). Additional technologies enable surveillance of songs as they move through the Internet. Referred to as "fingerprinting" or "hashes," these technologies let companies follow the locations of all encoded downloads on the Internet. Fingerprinting technologies can also recognize the fingerprint of a target computer and will only allow certain songs to play on the authorized equipment ("Partnership to Securely" 2003). "Metadata" tags also function like hashes in that they are hidden snippets of information embedded within many music files. Moreover, hashes also identify music files that have been traded on file sharing services as far back as May of 2000. Examining hashes is commonly used by the FBI and computer investigators in hacker cases ("Revealed: How RIAA Tracks Downloaders" 2003). These technologies enable the music industry to survey the manner in which consumers use audio files.

Fingerprinting technologies can also work in the opposite direction. They can help consumers quickly obtain information such as band and song names on Internet radio shows. The technology works quite simply. "The fingerprints are stored on a server. When the server is asked to identify a tune – for instance, a song playing on Internet radio – software matches a snippet of the tune, expressed in code, with the whole coded version of the song stored on the server" (Eisenberg 2003). Here, if a person hears a song she likes on her computer or cell phone, she can quickly identify names of commercial songs and artists by tapping into already set up databases. Whether or not there will be additional fees for the actual service and whether or not it may further decrease the number of human radio djs will be decided in the future. The companies involved in fingerprinting technology include Royal Philips Electronics, Shazam Entertainment in London, as well as Audible Magic in Los Gatos, California.

Regardless of how one examines fingerprinting technologies, the direct marketing implications are quite clear. Assuming that surveillance of the selections people fingerprint will also be a part of fingerprinting services, companies will be able to track and create databases containing every song consumers request to fingerprint. This information would then be valuable to record companies, which could then send individual advertisements to consumers based upon the kinds of music they fingerprinted. However, depending on how diverse music subscription services and radio station play lists will be, listeners may not be exposed to different music genres, hard-to-find releases, or music on independent labels. As a result, consumers may only receive certain kinds of music that are more commercialized than others, while at the same time, only receive advertisements for music within similar music genres. This system has potential to limit access to new kinds of music from other cultures, as well as close off access to different ideas and world views.

Indeed, these ideas have already been applied to the Internet through Sunstein's (2001) "me-oriented" society, where the personalization of information can limit exposure to different world views. They have also been applied to the advertising industry's method of segmentation through media, which may negatively affect audiences by making them less empathetic for people of different races, cultures or ideological backgrounds (Turow 1997). This "me-oriented" focus is already happening on digital cable television's Now Music Choice, which provides music for forty audio music channels, but is expanding into music videos, as well as video on-demand. The channels will track each user's music video choices in order to air specific commercials based on consumer selections (Hansell 2004d). This example suggests the "personalization" of information is only beginning to be applied to the music industry.

This advertising future where each household is given a different commercial obviously empowers advertising. It may create less empathy for other people (Sunstein 2001), as well as create potentially embarrassing situations for others. Imagine going over a friend's house to watch television, only to find all of the commercials geared toward diaper use, hemorrhoids, or other embarrassing health-related cases.

Even though marketers are trying to persuade consumers into purchasing music that appears similar to their own interests, not all music fans are interested in this marketing approach. Several enthusiasts have begun a grass-roots cyber public sphere of sorts where they exchange hardcopy mix CDs full of bands they've never heard of before. There has been an increasing number of "Mix of the month clubs" around the Internet, such as *www.crabwalk.com/CDmom,* or *www.artofthemix.org,* which enable people to connect and exchange new music though the mail (Gallagher 2003).

DRM AND HARDWARE

Besides offering new opportunities for copyright protection, surveillance and direct marketing, like the first two levels of digital rights management, the third level of copyright protection is embedded within audio hardware. Electronics manufacturers such as Sony and Nokia are now installing DRM systems into new stereo systems and hand-held devices to ensure that copyrighted materials cannot be reproduced and transferred from device to device ("Self-Destruct Files" 2003). DRM is also being applied to video game systems that play music. For example, "Song Pro," a cartridge that transfers digital music into Game Boy video game systems, is also using this technology (Marriott 2003). Additional manufactures of various audio hardware are following suit. Consumers wanting to make an additional CD copy are finding that not only will the CD not copy, but the hardware they use won't allow copying either.

Although these digital rights management technologies are in the process of being refined, there have been a number of limitations, which question their effectiveness. For example, a group of German hackers have already beaten the Key2audio encryption, while some copyproof compact disks have playback problems which prevent them from being played in a number of home and car stereos. Other hackers successfully removed four different kinds of watermarks developed by Verance, Blue Spike, CRL and Samsung/MarkAny in 2000 (Hardy 2000b). Watermarks enable labels to track files online. Finally, some upper end CD-Rom drives are able to correct errors encoded in the music enabling the encrypted CDs to be played on actual computers (Fenton 2001).

Nonetheless, anyone should be able to copy a copyproof CD by purchasing digital recording software and hardware. They will have to record the music in real time until newer technology is released. The concept is similar to recording a CD to tape, but the tape is the hard drive of the computer enabled by the recording software. One would need to play the CD while recording the audio live into the program. Then one could burn the music to disc after separating the recording into individual tracks based on the songs. Prices for these devices range from roughly $300 to the tens of thousands of dollars.

In sum, labels are using new technology to increase revenue by protecting their copyright holdings to such an extent that it appears to violate the fair use clause in the U.S. Constitution. Consumers will face increasing difficulties in making copies for themselves. In addition, the effect of these trends regulates consumers' experiences by limiting the manner in which music is consumed. Either by portability, location, or medium, DRM technologies affect how and where people can listen to music. To escape these copying limitations, consumers will need to purchase additional hardware and software to be able to copy copyproof CDs.

A NEW POLICING ROLE FOR MUSIC INDUSTRY

Besides working to prevent consumers from being able to exchange copies of CDs through various digital rights management technologies, the RIAA has taken a particular fondness to people exchanging music files over the Internet. The RIAA has been extremely successful at shutting down Web sites with music files through legal intimidation since the invention of Napster. Some 15,000 Web sites holding more than 300,000 copyrighted music files were shut down through 2001 and more continue to be shut down (Pohlmann 2001). In addition, the RIAA is working to change the legal system in order to force Internet providers to handover the names of file sharing suspects. It has also influenced the Justice Department with its creation of an intellectual task force in March of 2004 to increase criminal prosecutions for "illegal" music downloaders and copyright infringers (Schwartz 2004). Moreover, it is also disrupting networks and Web sites enabling peer-to-peer file sharing, as well as turning to policing tactics aimed to further prevent sharing of digital music files and music pirating.

While the music industry uses legal intimidation against file sharing Web sites such as Kazaa, Grokster, and eDonkey, it also focuses on software users instead of the actual software as being illegal, which means the music industry is shifting gears into a pseudo-policing organization. This change into using new policing tactics is largely the result of a federal judge's decision in Los Angeles, who ruled that Grokster and Morpheus, two file trading services, could be used for legal and illegal activities, similar to a Xerox machine. Therefore, the owners of the software were not liable for copyright infringement (Harmon 2003d). As a result of this 2003 ruling, the music industry expanded its sights from central servers like Grokster, eDonkey, and Kazaa, to individuals who download music in its pursuit of wiping out all illegal file sharing. In fact, industry officials were "preparing to pursue some of the millions of people who infringe copyrights using the Internet" (Harmon 2003b).

The industry may be able to do this more easily given another recent judicial decision forcing an Internet service provider to give up information on a subscriber. A federal judge's decision to order Verizon Communications to give a record company trade group the identity of an individual suspected of making available unauthorized copies of several hundred songs will help the industry curb file sharing. According to a spokesperson from ISP Earthlink, who also received subpoenas from the RIAA asking to identify individuals, "It is our intention to do so . . . [but] we disagree with the method that is being used here and while we support the right of them to enforce copyright, we think this is the wrong method for doing so" ("Record labels" 2003). The ruling suggests ISPs cannot guarantee the privacy of their subscribers and will eventually have to hand over personal use information even if its users are "suspected" of doing activity conceived as illegal.

In fact, the RIAA has been going after a lot of individuals as of 2003, when it asked for 850 subpoenas in U.S. District Court in Washington, D.C. (Ralis 2003). Around the same time, the RIAA was also getting the approval of roughly seventy-five subpoena applications a day, which forced the U.S. district court in Washington to reassign employees to help process the additional paperwork. In some cases, the subpoenas cite as few as five music files as "representative recordings" of music available for downloading from these users (Hardy 2003b). In March of 2004, the RIAA sued 532 people for illegally sharing digital music files over the Internet. Some lawsuits included individuals using computer networks at twenty-one universities ("RIAA Sues 532" 2004). On August 31st, 2004, the RIAA again brought copyright infringement lawsuits against 744 people ("RIAA Steps Up" 2004), while earlier in the same week the RIAA filed 506 copyright infringement lawsuits against other alleged file sharers ("RIAA Brings New Round" 2004).

During this time there were more than 7,000 lawsuits in North America and Europe and "There's going to be more litigation to come in more countries in 2005" according to IFPI Chairman/CEO John Kennedy (Koranteng 2005a). These changes expanded globally in 2005 with the IFPI making legal cases against 963 people for illegal downloading in Europe and Japan (Legrand and Van Gool 2005). Total cases against individuals accused of downloading or uploading illegal Internet music files was at 11,552 as of April 2005. Must of the cases were in the United States, but the industry continues to expand beyond the U.S. and Europe with its litigation.

Besides litigation, the music industry is also working on intimidating and frustrating people out of sharing music files. While the RIAA is suspected of deliberately placing mislabeled, truncated, or sonically messed up versions of popular songs on services like Kazaa in order to frustrate users out of using these peer-to-peer networks (Pogue 2003), file sharers are also discovering other unpleasant surprises. The RIAA began a campaign in 2003 aimed at making the lives of fans who swap music online even more uncomfortable. Amidst reports that the music industry was planning on hacking into personal computers of file swappers (Klinkenborg 2003), the RIAA began sending direct messages to people trading music files. These intrusive messages told file swappers "When you brake the law, you risk legal penalties. There is a simple way to avoid that risk: DON'T STEAL MUSIC" (Harmon 2003d C1). The music industry was to send at least a million of these messages into personal computers a week.

While legal decisions and tactics aimed at curbing file swapping may have an effect on some users, they cannot completely stop the activity. The music industry's methodology for dealing with file sharing has moved beyond these measures into a role of law enforcement. This newfound policing role has also been outsourced to institutions such as public and private universities. The music industry has been bombarding university administrators with complaints documenting alleged copyright infringement over their computer networks. As a result of the industry's complaints, several universities have also taken on a new surveillance and policing role concerning Internet usage.

For example, Harvard University warned undergraduates they would lose their Internet access if they illegally shared copyrighted material more than once over the Internet. Penn State deprived 220 students of their Internet connections after finding they were sharing copyrighted material. In addition, the United States Navel Academy punished eighty-five students who were found to have downloaded copyrighted songs and movies through the Academy's Internet connection. These incidents have led university administrators to consider campus-wide licenses for legal online music services (Harmon 2003c).

In addition, the RIAA has filed lawsuits against a small, but growing number of college students involved in file swapping sites. Although these lawsuits resulted in each student paying between $12,000 and $17,000 out of court ("EFF On College" 2003), the original lawsuits were much higher registering in the billion dollar range. Some of these college students' Web sites allowed their dorm residents, up-to 8,500 people depending on the dorm, access to a number of music files (Harmon 2003c).

If the RIAA gets its way, Internet users who allow people to copy music from their hard drives could eventually spend time in prison under additional legislation introduced by Michigan Rep. John Conyers and California Rep. Howard Berman. It is also possible they may eventually get their computers destroyed as well. The RIAA tried to add a clause in the federal anti-terrorism bill of 2001 to grant them immunity to "disable" computers of file traders, but the language was rejected by the Senate Judiciary Committee. More recently, Senator Orrin Hatch favored developing technology that would remotely destroy computers used for illegal downloads ("Senator: Trash" 2003). Although for the moment this may seem unreasonable, Conyers and Berman are in the process of creating legislation that may be worse. The proposed Conyers-Berman bill operates out of the assumption that each song or "copyrighted work" made available though a computer network would be copied at least ten times by others, which equals a total retail value of $2,500. As a result, their bill would move file sharing from a misdemeanor to felony, carrying a sentence of up to five years in jail ("Bill would" 2003). Smith's Piracy Deterrence and Education Act of 2003, HR 2570, also calls for "The U.S. attorney general to ensure that any unit of the DOJ (Department of Justice) responsible for investigating computer hacking or intellectual property crimes would be assigned 'at least one agent' to deal with copyright infringement" (Holland and Garrity 2003). This bill would permit the FBI to send cease-and-desist letters to infringers.

The RIAA also hired Bradley Buckles, director of Alcohol, Tobacco, Firearms and Explosives to head its Anti-Piracy Unit in 2003. His bureau held more than 4,800 employees with an $800 million dollar budget (Holland 2003). Indeed, the entertainment companies, including the Big 4 were also able to get the FBI to use its official logo and name on their DVDs, CDs, and other media in hopes the labels will deter people from making a copy or two.

While the RIAA has been effective in having universities and law enforce-ment "police" citizens' online activity and influence legislation, it is also em-ploying undercover investigators to bring cases to the police. These investigators are often former police officers, which can aid communication processes with real police officers. The RIAA has accompanied police in both New York and California on raids and search warrants (Lannert 1999). The RIAA has also as-sisted the U.S. Secret Service in conducting raids on additional counterfeiters (Horwitz 2002). In addition, the RIAA also donates more than $200,000 a year to fund NYPD activities aimed at stopping their merchandise from being pirated (Gardiner 2003). The New York City Police Foundation raised roughly $10 mil-lion a year in recent years through additional corporate donations. These private donations raise a number of ethical questions concerning the focus and role of public police departments in a democratic country. According to Jacqueline Helfgott, associate professor of criminal justice at Seattle University, "The po-lice belong to the public . . . hey don't belong to the rich and they don't belong to the companies. So when you get the companies paying money to ensure that certain laws are enforced, it creates a lot of ethical problems" (Gardiner 2003). Indeed, the effects of this disturbing trend surely go deeper than what the music industry has done.

By shaping the agendas of some law enforcement agencies, public protec-tion is turned into a privatized "pay-per-arrest" system where wealthy organiza-tions influence priorities of a publicly owned agency. Private organizations such as multi-national corporations have the privilege of being able to fund private investigations into "illegal" activity that can potentially diminish profits. They then report the illegal activity to the police. The unfortunate effect of this system is that people who cannot afford to pay for private investigations are at a disad-vantage. Poor people cannot afford to hire investigators to lobby and protect their interests and will be less likely to be able fund investigations into white-collar corporate or government crime.

IMPACT OF FILE SHARING

The justification for litigation concerning file sharing is simple. Since the suc-cess of Napster, the music industry has frequently argued that the illicit use of new technologies, such as unregulated peer-to-peer networks, have undermined CD sales and caused a marked slump in industry profits. Not surprisingly statis-tics presented by the RIAA and the IFPI claim an anecdotal relationship between a drop in sales and piracy (IFPI; RIAA). Recent academic literature regarding the intersection of new technology and the music industry often relates to this allegation, routinely yielding mixed results.

Some empirical analyses lend support to the general claim that digital downloads reduce sales (Liebowitz 2005; Peitz and Waelbroek 2004; Hong 2004; Zenter 2003). However, other researchers argue that downloads have had little to no discernable effect (Gayer and Shy 2005; Oberholzer-Gee and Strumpf 2005). Stevens and Sessions (2005) argue that downloads have decreased hardcopy demand since 2000, but overall consumption of recorded music has increased. Yet the debate is not limited to the basic empirical assertion that new technology and subsequent piracy are single-handedly responsible for decreased industry revenues. Other factors (as described in Chapter 6) such as less investment in new talent, fewer releases, a weak economy, increased prices, the emergence of other competing forms of entertainment, and the end of the cassette to CD media cycle all have been implicated in reduced sales (Freedman 2003; Langenderfer and Kopp 2004).

Surveys are noting fewer people are downloading music than originally expected, which counters claims made by the RIAA. Further research suggests there are more younger people purchasing music online, while most of the public believes downloading music should not be illegal. The RIAA appears to have over exaggerated financial loses resulting from file sharing through a public relations campaign, which effectively convinced journalists, who also mostly work for conglomerate corporations. According to a well-known study by Felix Oberholzer-Gee of Harvard Business School and Koleman S. Strumpf of the University of North Carolina at Chapel Hill, there is no effect between downloading and CD sales (Schwartz 2004).

Recent data also suggest a relatively small percentage of people aged 34 years and above download music while an increasing number of younger people are deciding to purchase music over the Internet. An April 2003 Ipsos-Reid study noted few people above 34 years of age have actually downloaded music. Only 14 percent of people in this age group have downloaded music. The poll also notes the number decreased to 12 percent with even fewer people downloading music in December of 2002 ("Death of the Disc?" 2003). Surprisingly, the most powerful group of music buyers is made up of people over thirty-four years old. America's eighty-one million thirty-five to fifty-four-year-olds outnumber the nation's seventy-five million fifteen to thirty-four year-olds, according to 2000 consensus figures ("Death of the Disc?" 2003). This demographic group not only has more cash to spend than younger people, it also views music more as a material item that can be placed in a library. Younger people may not view music in this manner because they may often simply download music and do not desire the hardcopy version of the CD or the accompanying artwork and case.

Whereas older people are less likely to download music and more likely to purchase hardcopies of CDs, younger people are more likely to download music. However, are younger people not purchasing music as a result? According to Nielsen/NetRatings, the global standard for Internet audience measurement, rap music is the most popular genre of music purchased by users downloading music ("Rap, Dance/Club" 2003). The rap and R&B market is also the most popular music genre generating 25 percent of all music sales (Hardy 2003a). In addition, 22 percent of the active Internet population aged fifteen to thirty-four, "downloaded music in the past thirty days and 71 percent of this audience purchased music in the past three months" ("Rap, Dance/Club" 2003). That means that 16.5 million people in this age group purchased music in a three-month period during the Spring of 2003. This suggests that younger people continue to purchase music even if they download it as well.

According to another study by market research group NPD, 60 percent of music consumers with access to the Web have not downloaded any music over the Internet for free, while sales of these same people were off by roughly 7 percent during the first quarter of 2003 ("Declining Music" 2003). This sales decline essentially mirrors the overall decline in music sales anyways. In fact, Russ Crupnick, Vice President of the NPD Group notes "Our research shows that even if digital file sharing were to disappear tomorrow, the record labels and retailers would still need to overcome important underlying causes of recent market declines" ("Declining Music" 2003).

While the RIAA claims it is losing money and that file sharing is illegal, large numbers of the public tend to disagree with the music industry's argument that downloading files should be considered stealing. According to one survey, 78 percent of Internet users who download music do not believe they are stealing (Pew Internet and American Life Project 2000). The public's perception of downloading music seems to parallel its notion of home taping. In a 1988 survey done by the Office of Technology Assessment (OTA) of the U.S. Congress, four out of ten Americans were counted as having taped recorded music in the previous year. It also noted that Americans tape-recorded individual musical pieces over 1 billion times per year. Much of the taping came from records or compact discs to audiocassettes to be played in cars or portable cassette players (Office of Technology Assessment 1989). The OTA found that the public, which consisted of people who taped music, as well as people who did not tape music, believed it acceptable to copy recorded music for one's own use or to give to a friend as long as the copies were not sold (Office of Technology Assessment 1989).

In fact, data on home taping suggest people who did a lot of home taping in the 1980s were also heavy buyers of music (Hardy 2000a). The music industry did not lose substantial amounts of money during the 1980s due to home taping. In fact, the industry's value increased dramatically mostly due to the invention of the compact disc. Given that the RIAA is now arguing that file sharing will damage CD profits, similar to what home taping could have done in the 80s, one needs to question this claim. Data suggest that Napster may have increased album sales, given the growth of U.S. CD album sales into 2000. It is possible that the people who used Napster were also the people who were more likely to purchase large amounts of music.

Indeed, many music downloaders purchase a fair amount of the music they sample online. According to a Pew Center Study (Pew Internet and American Life Project 2000), 21 percent of online music consumers say they ended up buying the music on CD or cassette "most of the time." Another 29 percent say they bought the music on a CD or cassette "some of the time," while 19 percent noted they bought the music on a CD or cassette "only a few times." Finally, 26 percent of music downloaders say they have never bought a CD or cassette of the music they have downloaded.

Another study of some 2,300 online music users by Jupiter Communications found that Napster users were 46 percent more likely to have increased their music purchasing habits than were online music fans who didn't use the service. Napster users were also 52 percent less likely to have decreased purchasing music than online music fans who did not use the service. As a result, all kinds of music online appeared more likely to spur than hamper sales (Gillen 2000).

Ultimately when members of the public are allowed to join together and work organically free of state or private commercial interests, as with some of the first file sharing services, they are seen as a threat to corporate America. As a result, the music industry felt a need to disrupt an organic, bottom-up public sphere in order to further consolidate its hold over the distribution of culture. It blames file sharing for sales loses, even though music downloading appears to be having a minimal impact on revenue. The irony is that the industry does not appear to be losing much money given that its projected revenue continues to increase, which will make it the highest in the history of the music industry's existence. In addition, what may be just as striking about the discussion concerning digital rights management, is that the RIAA has been extremely effective in terms of shaping the debate. The discussion has always placed the industry as the victim of music downloaders and away from other economic factors indicated in Chapter 5. The results of good public relations work have eschewed discussion away from the manner in which most musicians receive little profits from their work within the system set up by the major record labels. In addition, the music industry's influence on the legal system also fares negatively for the hierarchy of values placed within the law. People who download music may eventually get prison terms, while political leaders or corporations involved in war crimes, slavery, or genocide are given amnesty or immunity from prosecution.

CONCLUSION

This chapter focused on the music industry's response to challenges in copyright infringement. It began by examining the notion of fair use and how it plays out in the debate on file sharing and CD copying. It then described the music industry's success in influencing the legal system through its political lobby group, which has been able to write laws, support new forms of digital rights management technologies, as well as manipulate various political platforms in its favor. Because the public's reception to these new laws and technologies has not been warm, the music industry then transformed itself into a pseudo-policing organization in its pursuit of counter fitters and file traders. Although these industry pursuits assumed large numbers of people are illegally downloading music, recent surveys suggested the opposite. This chapter argued the music industry has been using its wealth and political influence to manipulate the legal system in its favor, while using fear of arrest as a means of forcing people into subscribing to "legitimate," or Big 4 supported music services, where more profit can be made compared to hardcopy sales. Besides creating fear, the music industry also wanted to "educate" the public and to " . . . deliberately confuse the organized mass duplication of pirated music with individual consumption and non-profit exchange of unlicensed music so as to secure more favorable forms of copyright protection" (Freedman 2003). These changes were initially planned and initiated not when the industry was losing money, but when sales were at an all time high. The result of these industry tactics questioned not only constitutionally protected notions of fair use, but the public's ability to operate free from government and private interests in the online world.

CHAPTER 8

THE RACE TO ONLINE DISTRIBUTION

While chapter 7 examined various legal and technological initiatives pursued by the music industry concerning digital rights management (DRM) and their impact on consumers, this chapter continues examining the digital realm by focusing on the music industry's transition into online distribution. It focuses on the impact of the Big 4's transition into the online world of digital music sales for consumers and retail while examining the connections the Big 4 are making with ISPs, Web sites that offer music downloads for sale, as well as with hardware and software manufacturing companies. This transition at first fueled further industry consolidation at the distribution level, but later expanded to incorporate a broad range of tangentially related businesses.

Besides describing the tiered system of online music subscription services and how ownership of music plays through them, this chapter also examines the differences between the services and what they mean for public access to online digital music. Consumers now need to subscribe to several different services in order to fully access a variety of tunes because each service offers different labels and exclusive content. Finally, this chapter also looks at the impact of the Big 4's entry into online sales on traditional retail stores and their reaction to this transition. Although some companies may be better positioned than others in the transition into the online world of music sales, the battle being waged within the music industry is between retailers, distributors, and record compa-

nies for online music sales. The race between all parties will be to establish online name recognition and/or ownership of various Internet providers and online
ventures.

This chapter argues the Big 4's transition into digital music sales is giving
the music industry more control over online musical culture, more profits when
compared with hardcopy formats, as well as more revenue as it begins to take
away profits once associated with traditional retail. Moreover, because of industry consolidation, the few companies that control the music industry are working
together to create an architecture for online music sales that forces consumers
into purchasing a number of different services in order to have access and to
purchase music. These actions are extensions of the music industry's business
plan to divide music through various formats, video games, new media and
hardware. Therefore, the music industry is creating a divide between consumers
who will have money to pay for various subscription services and overpriced
digital downloads, from those who cannot afford to have access.

MOVING CONSUMERS ONLINE

The drive to push people online was at first slow, but it eventually took hold,
and fairly quickly given the immense difficulty of introducing a new medium.
Indeed, the music industry was reported to have invested $2 billion in planning
and developing online music initiatives (Benz 2002), which appears to have
began before the industry experienced a drop in hardcopy sales. It is likely they
invested even more, whereas some estimates put their investment closer to $4
billion. The music industry's plan for going online was at least four-fold. First, it
wanted to give the public the option to purchase individual tracks and albums
online, but at higher profit margins. Second, it wanted to offer some digital
tracks for sale online before they were available in other formats. That way the
industry can get at least "2 sales" out of certain songs. Third, the industry
wanted to create subscription services where consumers have to pay to access
and purchase music and last, it wanted to divide music through various labels
and exclusive content throughout a number of online distribution services. This
division would then force people to pay for more than one service to access a
variety of labels and artists.

So far, the business model seems to be working quite well for the music industry. In terms of weekly digital track sales, they went from a little over
200,000 in July of 2003, to more than 2.4 million a year later (Garrity 2004d).
Digital sales are now expected to outgrow hardcopy sales. In addition, income
from music subscription services is also expected to outgrow download sales by
2008 according to industry research firm Jupiter Research (Garrity and Banerjee
2004). Subscription service revenue in 2003 was $113 million per year and is
expected to grow to $700 million by 2008 (Garrity and Banerjee 2004). If the
numbers continue as projected, the music industry will have been successful in

changing the manner in which people around the world consume music. What is even more interesting is that the music industry was able to accomplish this without their input.

Nonetheless, the road to online victory was probably not as easy as initially planned. During the late nineties there were over 120 online companies, several of them music-related, which ended up going out of business due to poor planning and the shake up of the dot.com bubble ("Music-related dotcoms" 2001). Stocks in dot.com music businesses bottomed out toward the end of 2000 amid fears of file swapping, lack of profits on digital music services, poor business planning and a weakened advertising climate. According to Billboard magazine, "Start-up Internet music companies, along with some parent companies of the major labels and many retailers, wholesalers and distributors, posted double-digit percentage declines from a year ago, with many stocks trading at near 52-week lows at the close of 2000" (Garrity 2001a). Popular sites like MP3.com and Musicmaker.com, which were heavily invested in by the Big 4, saw their shares decline by over 80 percent during this time period (Garrity 2001a). In addition, stock performances by parent companies also declined. Shares in parent company Time Warner closed down 26 percent from the year before while Sony's stock declined by 50 percent. Musicland was one of the few retailers that did enjoy a boost to its stock during this time mostly because it was purchased by Best Buy (Garrity 2001a).

Other online music ventures such as Reciprocal, Supertracks, Hithive, Uplister, Music.com, and Musicbank all disappeared due to little investment and minimal business after the bubble broke. At the same time, the Big 4 gobbled up industry vanguards such as MP3.com, Emusic.com, Launch Media, Myplay, and Napster. UMG bought former rival MP3.com for more than $300 million, purchased Emusic.com and carved out a 50 percent ownership in GetMusic, while Bertelsmann acquired digital locker service myplay.com and merged it with online retailer CDnow (Garrity 2001f). During the shake-out of 2001, conglomerates emerged as the true victors mostly due to their immense pocketbooks, which often enables them to weather difficult times. The shake-out also spurred immense consolidation. As of 2003, the field had been reduced to only six major digital music retailers. Their victory assured that online music sales would be geared toward the bottom-line interests of the Big 4 over consumer interests.

However, the trend toward consolidation within online distributors reversed itself briefly after 2003 with importance being placed on rights to access music, service fees, and profit margins. As long as the Big 4 could regulate these components in their favor, it would not need to control every site that sold music downloads online. As a result, a boom for digital retailing occurred after the initial consolidation. Amazon.com, Circuit City, Virgin Megastores, Wal-Mart, Starbucks, and everyone else raced to establish themselves as digital retailers for at least two reasons. First, they moved here because they could make money and second, because of the fear that the industry would not manufacture hardcopy CDs in the future. On a side note, online digital music retailing continues to increase because several of these sites are often the only place to find new releases. Consumers may not have a choice if they want quick access to new releases.

Indeed, the Big 4 appear to be moving toward a digital-only future, which they hope will increase revenue and control over music consumption. EMI has already outsourced its compact disc and DVD production, while other companies are going in this direction as well (Timmons 2004). It is likely they will begin to focus on digital-only labels and releases. In fact, there is evidence that Universal is already doing this though its creation of its digital only label, Universal Music Enterprises Digital. Universal will make 75 percent of the online profits in exchange to market and cross-promote the music on its label and license it in film and television shows (Leeds 2004c). Digital Musicworks International is also a new digital-only label whose roster includes Dwight Twilley, Red Light Music, and other artists (Banerjee 2004f). Warner Music Group is also thinking about creating a digital-only label.

With digital-only labels, manufacturing, packaging, mailing, and other costs-associated with hard-copy products are eliminated. In addition, digital-only formats also force consumers into purchasing music through subscription services, which increases revenue. Finally, these changes may negatively affect retail store profits. Selling digital singles through services owned or invested in by the Big 4 will redirect the money that would have gone to independent stores and retail chains back to the major labels.

Another way to move people into subscription services is to cross-promote online. The music industry is doing this by teaming up with ISPs to co-own and cross-promote their music services. Lycos and Yahoo! were the first Web portals to connect their users with various music subscription services, while AOL continues its blatant cross-promotion of its own musical artists. Other music-related companies are in the process of teaming up with ISPs like Sony and UMG did with Yahoo! in order to have the ISPs cross-promote their music services. In AOL/Time Warner's case, it owns the ISP service and its music site, which allows it to easily cross-promote the music from its own labels. BMI and Emusic linked to each other's Web sites, traded banner ads and jointly conducted listening polls, while Emusic also allowed BMI artists to use its Artist Uplink service, a Web site creation tool (Grebb 2000).

Internet portals may easily turn into the next broadcast or cable television. Therefore, ownership and the ability to advertise, cross-promote and collect advertising dollars through them is extremely important to the conglomerate music industry. The flipside to cross-promotion is non-conglomerate affiliated artists are often sidelined, while ISPs can turn into self-serving promotional and commercial communications devices given the current ownership. Nonetheless, one can still see several examples of exclusive music and other music-related content in Internet portals, which add to the trend of separating more and more exclusive music through a variety of outlets in the music industry. In 2005, AOL exclusively Webcasted the Live 8 concerts, but this time, viewers did not need an AOL account. Yahoo! Music also had a different version of the former TV show "Pepsi Smash," which included exclusive music performances and other content designed only for Yahoo! (Bruno and Garrity 2005).

ONLINE SERVICES: SO MANY RELATIONSHIPS, SUCH LIMITED COMPATIBILITY

Chart 4 describes a few dominant online ventures where consumers can access and own digital downloads. While they are characterized by historically amorphous corporate partnerships and structures, most remain co-owned by the Big 4 and software manufacturers. All services operate with various levels of cost and each service offers access to different labels, which may or may not be included in the other services. Most services charge customers through a tiered system allowing paying music fans different levels of access to music. For example, typical services may charge roughly ten dollars a month for unlimited downloads, but consumers will not be allowed to burn the songs onto a CD or transfer the tunes onto a portable unit.

Almost all of the online services are subscription based. Therefore one has to pay even if not listening to music. Each service allows consumers different degrees of access to music depending on how much they pay. The most basic level of access, which is also the least expensive option, enables consumers to simply hear music while their computer is online. This option is essentially like listening to a radio, but the music is coming from a computer and subscribers have to pay for it. However, unlike broadcast radio, which can be recorded on a cassette tape, most elemental online subscription-based music options do not allow the music to be recorded. Subscribers need to pay more for this option. Nonetheless, commercials are nonexistent, unless embedded within the actual songs.

The next level of access allows people to listen to songs on their computers for playback even when they are not online. However, if one's subscription to the service expires, so do the downloads. They fade away into unusable data files. Corporations call these "temporary," "conditional," or "tethered" downloads. With this option, consumers are allowed to "rent" music, but they are not allowed to own it, meaning they are not allowed the freedom to make copies, or move the music to another device for playback.

The most expensive option for consumers does enable limited forms of music ownership. This is in the form of "portable" or "permanent" downloads, meaning consumers are allowed to burn a CD copy of these songs. However, in most cases, one cannot store these files in more than 3 computers or email the files. Nonetheless, it is possible to get around this limitation by burning a CD of the songs and then placing them back in the hard drive as standard MP3 files, which will provide consumers with more control over the ownership of their music. Consumers can then transfer the files into portable devices or make more duplicate CDs.

The Big 4 advantage of owning or investing in online music subscription services is important to note. The profits accrued from subscription services are divided between the record labels and the online services, which are also usually invested in or owned by the record labels anyways. This means non-Big 4 owned online stores end up paying between sixty-five to seventy cents to the record companies for each 99-cent item sold (Hansell 2004c). By setting the standard rate for downloads, the Big 4 were able to assure they would receive a good share of the profits, even if they did not own the Web site that sold the music.

MUSICAL CHAIRS

In 2003, the New York Times listed five major online digital music providers including MusicNow, MusicNet, PressPlay, RealOne Music Pass and Listen.com's Rhapsody ("Data Provided" 2003). As of November 2005 MusicNow was owned by AOL (which still has an on going partnership with Apple to provide service to AOL subscribers). The service is now AOL MusicNow and old MusicNow subscribers must transfer their accounts to maintain access to their "rented" music libraries. Roxio bought PressPlay and recently relaunched the service as Napster, and RealOne MusicPass is now one with Rhapsody. Yahoo! launched its own music subscription service buying MusicMatch and partnering with MusicNet.

Pressplay (now Napster) has enjoyed a number of investments from various hardware, software and music industry companies. Yahoo!, Microsoft, Universal Music Group, Sony Music Entertainment, and Roxio have all at one time "owned" or invested in Pressplay. Roxio, which is best known for CD-recording software now seems to dominate its ownership. Roxio also makes software that enables consumers to capture, edit and burn photos, videos, or music onto CDs or DVDs. When it purchased into Pressplay, Roxio positioned itself to connect the online music on its site to its software. By purchasing services or software like Roxio, consumers would be able to listen to music and participate in other online multi-media activities. It's estimated worth was $30 million in 2003 (Carter 2003).

Roxio also purchased Napster's name after it filed for bankruptcy and eventually reintroduced Pressplay under the Napster banner. Both UMG and Sony still own stakes in Roxio. By cross-promoting the music sites with Yahoo!'s service as well, UMG was also in a nice position along with its partnership of twenty-eight music retailers and other Web sites to offer several of the 43,000 songs it owned for purchase and download ("Universal Music" 2003). Besides owning Emusic.com and MP3.com, UMG also owned GetMusic and Farm Club Internet sites. They provided music downloads with partners such as America Online, USA Networks, and MTV, which provided promotional services ("Universal Music" 2003). Sony Music Entertainment also invested in a number of Internet Companies such as: Listen.com, MusicNet, The Platform Network, and Yupi.com ("Sony Music" 2003). As time has passed, many of these less known sites changed ownership or disappeared all together due to declining investment, poor business strategies and minimal consumer interest.

While PressPlay was originally owned by UMG, and Sony, another service known as MusicNet was formed by the other three Big 4-related record companies: AOL/Time Warner, Bertelsmann Music Group, and EMI ("BMG Entertainment" 2003; Harmon, 2003a). MusicNet was also co-owned by RealNetworks through its ties with Bertelsmann, while AOL planned to sell its part of MusicNet. RealNetworks also was to spend $36 million to acquire Listen.com, creator of Rhapsody.

Member numbers for these "legitimate" subscription services are dramatically increasing. According to one industry analyst, paid music services had no more than 350,000 subscribers in early 2003 ("Data provided" 2003). This number is nothing compared to the tens of millions that Napster and Kazaa once enjoyed. By 2004, RealNetworks had 550,000 subscribers, America Online's MusicNet had 260,000 and Musicmatch had 225,000 paying customers. Napster and Yahoo! did not report how many subscribers they had (Hansell 2004b). By 2005, Rhapsody indicated it had over 1 million subscribers, while Napster had over 40,000 (Bruno 2005e). There is no doubt the music industry is enjoying major growth with digital music sales through subscription services.

CHART 4: ONLINE DIGITAL MUSIC PROVIDERS						
	A	**B**	**C**	**D**	**E**	**F**
iTunes 2,000,000+ tracks	N	99¢	U	3-5	Y	MAC, PC (AAC)
MSN Music 1,000,000+ tracks	N	99¢	V	5	Y	PC (WMA)
Napster 1,000,000+ tracks	Y *	80-99¢	U	3	Y †	PC (WMA)
Rhapsody 1,000,000+ tracks	Y *	79-99¢	5	3	Y †	PC (limited iPod) (RAX), (WMA)
Yahoo! Music Unlimited 1,000,000+ tracks	Y *	79¢-99¢	7	3	Y †	PC (WMA)
AOL Music Now 1,000,000+ tracks	Y *	99¢	V	3	Y †	PC (WMA)
A. Subscription Fee *a la carte tracks available						
B. Cost Per Track						
C. Number of Burns per Track: Unlimited (U), Varies (V)						
D. Number of Computers (concurrent use)						
E. Mobile Devices † only with monthly subscription						
F. Compatibility & File Type: Advanced Audio Coding (AAC), Windows Media Audio (WMA), Real Audio 10 (RAX)						

Sources include: *www.itunes.com, www.napster.com, www.rhapsody.com, music.Yahoo!.com, aol.musicnow.com/az/home.jhtml?_requestid=105687* and email correspondence with customer service representatives from Rhapsody, iTunes, MSN Music(9 November 2005) and Yahoo!

The previous chart briefly outlines the services offered by major online digital music providers. These are fee-based services selling digital tracks and other digital content through licensing agreements with all four majors and various independent labels. Their catalogs vary from 800,000-2 million tracks, which are typically available for purchase a la carte or accessible by subscription. Single tracks average a dollar each for purchase, while subscription services, which allow a customer to "rent" songs, range from $5-10 per month. Rhapsody, Napster, Yahoo! Music Unlimited and AOL Music Now offer both services, while iTunes and MSN Music focus on a la carte sales.

In order to download "rented" tracks to portable devices, subscription services require increased monthly fees from $10-15. Purchased tracks can also be added to portable devices through subscription services for additional fees (around a dollar per track). Purchased tracks can be transferred from the hard-drives of licensed computers with non-subscription services to compatible portable devices. However, with some services, such as Rhapsody, purchased tracks are never saved to the hard drive of a computer, but must be burned directly to CD with Rhapsody supported software.

Actual ownership and usage of "purchased" tracks varies by provider. iTunes sells tracks in Advanced Audio Coding (AAC) format. These files can be used with iTunes for PC and Macs, but are only supported by iPods as a portable device. iTunes allows users to burn a purchased song to disc an unlimited number of times, but these tracks will only play on up to three computers at any one time, though users are allotted an unlimited number of iPods for portable listening. Playlists can only be burned up to seven times before they must be altered.

The remaining services use Windows Media Audio (WMA) file formats, with the exception of Rhapsody, which streams in WMA, but sells downloads in Real Audio 10 (RAX) format-DRM wrapped AAC files. This forces Rhapsody's users to play tracks on its software even after they have been purchased. Rhapsody limits the total number of times consumers are allowed to burn purchased songs to three times. Furthermore the service is not compatible with Mac operating systems. But like iTunes, the service allows the tracks or subscription service to function on multiple computers. The catch is that this is limited to three computers *at one time*. Users must "de-license" a computer before adding a new verified computer after the "simultaneous use" number has been reached. This often applies to portable devices as well, limiting usage on average to two devices, or even to a finite number of total transfers of a track to portable devices (around ten for AOL MusicNow). Rhapsody and Pressplay only enable users "to listen to songs they have downloaded only as long as they continue to pay for the service" (Flynn 2003), and at one point, none of the songs in Sony Music's catalog were burnable (Pogue 2003). Pressplay does allow consumers to copy their purchased songs to CD, a Sony minidisc player, or other portable music players. However, Pressplay will not allow music to be transferred to Apple's iPod. In other words, do not buy competitor's hardware if you use Pressplay.

With AOL's service, for $8.95, one can listen to an unlimited number of songs on demand through Internet streaming, which is very similar to listening to a radio station. For $15.00, one can download twenty songs per month and listen to another twenty at one time. However, for both services, subscribers cannot listen to AOL's music on more than two computers, nor can they copy the music to other devices or send the tunes to other people. A premium service of $17.95 a month allows users to burn ten songs a month onto a recordable CD, enabling the subscriber to do whatever he or she wants to do with the music (Hansell 2003). However, a typical CD costing roughly $15 often has fifteen-twenty songs on it, and owners can usually do anything they want with the music. So, if one wants the equivalent number of tunes that a twenty song CD has to offer for $15, one may have to pay roughly $40 through the AOL service. If one is interested in ownership and control of music, it is cheaper to simply buy the hardcopy CD, rather than download it from AOL's service.

Comparing all of the online music services, Apple seems the most "accessible" because it still does not charge a subscription fee to access or purchase its music. In 2001, Apple angered music industry executives when it began its "Rip, mix, burn" advertisement campaign, which encouraged people to duplicate CDs, create mix compilations and burn musical downloads. However, a few years later in 2003, its entry into digital music service was hailed as having "compatibility with a hardware product that is elegant and easy to use" according to Hillary Rosen, chief executive of the RIAA (Richtel 2003). Apple won over the hearts of the RIAA with its foray into online music distribution.

Apple also manufactures portable MP3 players, hardware that copies and transfers music, as well as software that reads it. The company is positioning itself to promote safe, easy, and legal access to online music in order to boost revenue though all of its holdings. Apple entered into the digital music service market with access to catalogs of the Big 4 labels and planed to sell individual songs for $.99 and albums for $9.99. Apple's service at first only allowed listeners to download tunes into their Macintosh computers through Apple's iTunes software, which also enabled users to transfer tracks into Apple's iPods for portable music. This ability was distinct because other services did not allow it. Apple's service also enabled users to create burned copies of CDs, where as other services usually did not allow this feature (Flynn 2003). It is likely that consumers will have to pay a subscription fee in the near future. Eddy Cue, vice president of Apple in charge of its iTunes division indicated Apple might consider turning itself into a subscription-based service (Hansell 2004c).

Apple at first allowed consumers to record up to ten CD copies per playlist, play the songs on up to three computers, as well as have access to artwork, videos and other content (Flynn 2003). However, according to the Electronic Frontier Foundation (2005), Apple can change at any time what consumers can do with the music they purchase from its online store. For example, it suddenly decreased the number of playlist copies consumers could make from ten to seven in 2004. Apple simply modified its DRM software, which then directly affected consumer behavior (Electronic Frontier Foundation (2005).

Apple will create a Windows version of its software in order to acquire a larger consumer base and expand the sales of iPods to other music fans who use

Windows. Indeed, Apple appears to have been the most successful online music service for downloading tunes given that consumers supposedly downloaded over two million songs within the first two weeks of service. In 2005, it also had over 80 percent of the digital music services market and roughly 75 percent of the portable music player market ("Music Stats Oct 6," 2005).

In short, Apple hopes that by moving into the digital music market it will be able to increase hardware sales while affiliating its brand with safe, legal and easy access to music downloading. By allowing consumers more freedom to use music how they want to, but from its inception, only through Apple's software and hardware, Apple hopes to increase sales of its computers, software and portable music devices. As a result, Apple's initial framework confined consumer choice to only one service and hardware manufacturer in order to establish long term retention given that the service was only likely to function with the appropriate combination of Apple-based software and hardware.

SUBSCRIPTION SERVICE LIMITATIONS AND EXCLUSIVES

While most services started out offering the same basic 250,000 songs because they had similar deals with the Big 4 records companies (Pogue 2003), each service also offered exclusive contracts with certain labels and artists. They continue to "compete" by offering specific songs only available on their services, or songs first available for preview on their service. Here is where we see the Big 4's business plan for online music sales pan out. For example, David Bowie's album "Hours," had an exclusive two-week period on the digital download market before it was available in retail stores. It also carried an extra song not available on the hardcopy form (Christman 1999). Amazon.com's digital music downloading service also offered exclusive tracks from Sarah McLachlan and Cheap Trick for free or for sale weeks before the street date release (Fitzpatrick 1999). In addition, Virgin artist Ben Harper released seven live tracks unavailable in physical form over the Internet for $1.99 per track, or $9.99 for the bundle (Christman 2000a). AOL also features exclusives through its service.

In addition, Pressplay was the only place with a licensing agreement with J Records, which featured artists such as Alicia Keys, Busta Rhymes, Tyrese, Rod Stewart, and others ("Pressplay Becomes" 2003). It was also the only service where consumers could find music from the film *Two Weeks Notice*. As a result, fans of Counting Crows and Vanessa Carlton, as well as other musicians had to subscribe to the service for access ("Sites + Sounds Newsline" 2002). Warner Music Group had Barenaked Ladies, Collective Soul, Mana, and Matchbox Twenty also offer Internet only exclusive tracks (Christman 2000c).

Rhapsody also provided exclusives. It offered Justin Timberlake's "Like I Love You" remix by Basement Jaxx, as well as an exclusive interview through its service. In addition, Rhapsody also unveiled new songs ahead of other online services. So far, Art Garfunkel and Bruce Hornsby were the first artists to be premiered through the service ("Sites + Sounds Newsline" 2002). Apple also used exclusives as a means to bring in more customers. Tom Petty provided two exclusive live tracks while Widespread Panic sold live downloads of two 2003 concerts exclusively through iTunes.

Yahoo!'s music site also sold exclusive downloads, as did the now defunct Musicmaker.com, which had an exclusive five-year licensing deal with the Zomba record labels (Olson 1999a, 1999b). The Rolling Stones' works on EMI were also available only through Rhapsody during the summer of 2003 ("The Rolling Stones" 2003). Finally, Elvis fans had to subscribe to the MusicNow service to access a new Elvis Channel, which was to offer the world's largest online catalog of Elvis songs among other media and information ("Elvis Fans" 2003). Napster also worked out a deal with UMG for a two week exclusive digital distribution of Tom Petty's catalog.

Here is yet another good example in support of the argument that the music industry is dividing access through several services, which not only costs more, but also enables repeat sales for the Big 4 labels. Sarah McLachlan made available her first single "Fallen" to iTunes before the actual album was released and then offered an exclusive live EP for 30 days. McLachlan's tune "Afterglow" was also promoted with an exclusive stream through Rhapsody. In addition, there was a live performance only through AOL.

Besides Big 4-owned online subscription services, more and more retail services are also using exclusives. For example, Wal-Mart's online music store offered exclusive music by Jessica Simpson, 3 Doors Down and Shania Twain in 2004 while it also noted it would be the exclusive supplier of songs from the Curb Records label, whose roster included Tim McGraw and LeAnn Rimes ("Wal-Mart Tunes" 2004).

However, consumers may also have problems finding some recent singles to download. According to a study cited in Billboard magazine, the biggest problem facing new digital music subscription services was their shortage of hit content (Garrity 2002a). MusicNet, Pressplay and Rhapsody on average contained only 10 percent of the top 100 singles and only 9 percent of the top 100 albums (Garrity 2002a). This was mainly a result of artist licensing and royalty issues. These artists or their agents were not interested in online sales, or they were in the process of negotiating contracts. Bands like The Red Hot Chili Peppers and Metallica were at first refusing to make their music available to some services such as Apple's iTunes service ("Pirate CD" 2003).

As mentioned earlier, the services, formats, and portable devises are not usually compatible, which may require users to purchase all new music if they lose their mobile player, or if they want to purchase a new one. Many online music services have songs in Microsoft's Windows Media Audio (WMA) DRM, which is not supported in a number of portable devices. Unlike MP3s, it is difficult to convert these kinds of DRM files into other formats, which will work in additional portable devices. On a similar note, if consumers decide to switch online music subscription services, they may also have to purchase a compatible listening device, since the format and DRM may not work in their current listening device. For example, RealNetworks was not happy when it learned the songs from its online store could not be transferred to Apple's iPod (Electronic Frontier Foundation 2005).

In essence, the evolving online music distributors, backed by the Big 4 with various hardware and software companies, are beginning the foray into the digital realm as a sort of limited pay-per-play radio. Here, subscribers pay to rent music, which in most cases infers they cannot own it depending on the amount of money they want to pay. Even then, the music they purchase is likely to be more expensive than the hardcopies they could purchase in retail stores. This "digital" radio station of sorts costs more than actual radio, but does not have commercials interrupting music.

Ultimately, the transition to online sales will allow the music industry to gain additional revenue by cutting into retail and distribution businesses. Because digital music distribution does not require the physical storage, or the manufacture of hardcopy CDs, cases, or artwork associated with actual CDs, labels will be able to generate additional revenue through these cost saving measures. Furthermore, by charging similar amounts of money for digital music as with hardcopy CDs, online music services allow the Big 4 to co-opt some of the money that would have originally gone to retail stores.

The music industry is also enabling two sales of the same product by releasing digital singles up to three months before the actual album is released. So fans may first buy the single, then later purchase the album, which also contains the previously released single, thus purchasing at least one song twice. Single sales also help the music industry by deciding if selling entire albums will be profitable. Data on consumers is easier for executives to track now that they know who is buying what, how much they're buying and when they buy it. This new distribution method aids the music industry in terms of how much money they will invest in artists and promotion.

Besides saving on manufacturing and distribution costs, the transition to download sales online also enables the labels to make even more money since they own stakes in almost every aspect of online sales. For example by investing in Roxio or RealNetworks, the content provider (meaning the music industry) is now in a position to own part of the means by which content is distributed. The labels are interested in owning the underlying technology used by content creators that creates and distributes digital content. RealNetworks develops and markets software products and services enabling users of personal computers and other consumer electronic devices to send and receive audio, video and other multimedia services using the Web. By investing in companies like Roxio that make software enabling CD or MP3 burning, the music industry is also positioning itself to own another means in which music is transferred and created. Labels now own part of the software that enables the creation of music on recordable compact discs. Unfortunately, while the labels increase their cut from online profits through new joint ventures with ISPs, middlemen and music sites, artists' cuts drop or stay the same. The following chart provides a break down of the income made from digital downloads.

DISTRIBUTION OF INCOME FROM DIGITAL DOWNLOAD SALES

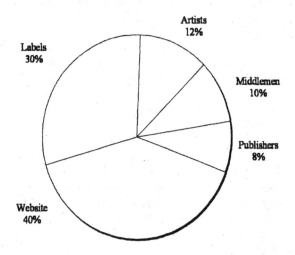

Chart 5: Source: Einhart 2003.

According to chart five, actual Web sites make the most money from sales of digital downloads. They make roughly 40 percent of the total sale. This is why the Big 4 invested in various Web sites that offer music. For example, Sony and UMG invested in Pressplay (via Roxio), while AOL/Time Warner, BMG, and EMI invested with MusicNet. Their investment strategy will position them to make a higher percentage of the money divided from sales. The labels then make 30 percent directly through "performance royalties" required to license the actual recording.

Percentage-wise, some artists make the same amount of money from CD sales, as they do from digital downloads. Some successful bands do negotiate better percentages than the 12 percent in chart five. However, these percentages are the result of several charges associated with actual manufacturing processes. According to music industry attorney Don Passman, the labels first take out 25 percent for the packaging deduction, then another 15-20 percent for a configuration deduction because the medium is a CD and not a cassette, and then another 15 percent for loosely defined "free goods" (Passman 2003). These percentages are taken out from the total amount, leaving 13-16 percent of the leftovers for the musician, which gives the labels a larger share, instead of taking out the artists' share at the same time as the other fees. For digital downloads, some companies are doing the same thing, meaning they are taking out all of the surcharges when packaging and configuration do not exist. Others are paying the full CD royalty without the configuration of the manufacturing reductions, which makes a substantial increase, possibly up to 50 percent, in how much an artist earns (Passman 2003). So far, UMG and WMG are not deducting these fees in digital singles sales (Garrity 2003b).

At this stage it is difficult for independent musicians to make connections with every online distributor or retailer. As a result, they usually go through middlemen who also take money in order to organize bulks deals with several Big 4 owned distributors and retail sites in order to make digital music sales easier for musicians. Other middlemen, who usually get 10 percent, are intermediaries between some music sites and consumers. For example, Liquid Audio, MusicNet, and Rhapsody sell their services through "middlemen," or secondary distributors like Amazon or AOL. So, not only will Warner Music Group make money from download sales, its parent company AOL will also earn money as the middleman. Finally, music publishers earn the last 8 percent of online sales through "mechanical royalties," or the amount to license the music. Again, most music publishing companies are also owned by the labels and the trend is to promote artists whose music and songwriting rights are owned by the label.

Unfortunately, online sales also create additional opportunities for companies to take even more money from musicians through interest and/or fraud. Digital distributors distribute profits from sales during different time periods. Some every month, some every three months, some every six months, and some every year. The time of the dispersals can enable companies to keep the interest accrued from digital sales. The system is also one of based on trust. Musicians have to trust what the companies tell them. However, exactly how many digital files were sold is more difficult to account for than with hardcopy CDs. In fact, they make mistakes.[1] One knows exactly how many CDs were manufactured, given away to radio stations and how many were sent to distributors and how many were sold. With digital distribution, there is more room for fraud.

In sum, the Big 4 are involved in monetary extraction in nearly every phase of download sales. Through various investment strategies, the music industry has successfully colonized the world of digital music sales while positioning itself for complete control over nearly every aspect of digitized music distribution. Instead of just making money from one service, by investing in a number of services that offer different labels and bands, online digital sales are evolving in a manner which forces people to subscribe to several services if they want to hear music from different artists and labels. Because they've invested in, owned by, or have financial contracts with nearly every service, the Big 4 have positioned themselves to profit from any of the services, while consumers will end up spending more money depending on how much access to music they want.

Moreover, the music industry influenced legislature to such an extent that consumers cannot resell digital music, where as they can resell hardcopy CDs. The 'first sale doctrine,' which enabled consumers to resell physical copies of music or DVDs, was rejected by Congress in 1998 for digital sales as a result of the DMCA ("US Copyright" 2001). As noted in the previous chapter, media industries helped write substantial portions of this law. The end of the first sale doctrine in the digital realm will generate additional revenue for the industry, since consumers are more likely to take risks on purchasing used CDs instead of newer ones given the cost difference. Consumers don't have this option in the digital world. This may negatively affect retail stores as well because used music can often bring in 10 percent of total sales. The used CD market in the U.S. had a retail value of $254 million per year in 2000 ("US Copyright" 2001).

IMPACT ON TRADITIONAL RETAIL OUTLETS

If the Big 4 labels successfully go online to bypass traditional retail outlets, it could easily mean the kiss of death for record and CD stores. In fact, this may already be happening. Two major retail chains, Wherehouse Entertainment and Value Music recently filed for Chapter 11 bankruptcy protection while nearly 500 music specialty stores around the United States had to shut down in between 2002 and 2003 ("Why Experts" 2003). Another estimate put more than 1000 music specialty stores as lost in 2003 (Christman 2004b). In addition, Southwest Wholesale, a one-stop/independent distributor closed, as did 275 Kmart stores, which also sold music (Christman 2003a). More will close in the future as the music industry forces people online, which will be the only place where consumers can access exclusive releases.

It is likely stores are closing because the industry is slowly sucking their profits away from them. Online music sales from industry-invested sites enable the Big 4 to tap into the $3-6 profit per CD traditionally set aside for distribution and retail. This trend of taking away money from retail is not a new one. According to Billboard retail analyst Ed Christman, the Big 4 took margin away from retailers when they introduced the new CD format in 1983. They left retailers with a gross margin of 35-36 percent as opposed to the 41-42 percent margin merchants enjoyed from vinyl and tape (Christman 2000b). If the major labels offer exclusive songs that are only found through their Internet subscription services, or they release the downloadable versions months before the retail version comes out, why should consumers go to retail stores if they don't have the latest releases and if they do not offer exclusive songs?

These recent bankruptcies and store closings are speeding up retail's efforts to distribute music online. As of 2003, six of the largest music retailers were planning to sell downloadable music on the Internet through a company called Echo (Holson 2003b). Echo planned to mirror Apple's pay-per-song model and promote it largely in the Windows world once it had the technology and the licensing deals ("Apple's online" 2003). Best Buy, the nation's number one electronics retailer, Tower Records, Virgin Entertainment Group, Wherehouse Entertainment, Hastings Entertainment, and Trans World Entertainment each own an equity stake in Echo making them majority owners.

Anderson Merchandisers, one of the largest magazine wholesalers and the music distributor to Wal-Mart, was also planning on becoming an online distributor of downloadable music in retail outlets (Bartels 2003). Anderson Merchandisers already owned assets of one of the first companies to deliver music online, Liquid Audio, which had a catalogue of 350,000 songs available for downloading. Anderson Merchandisers hoped to unveil a massive plan to cross-promote downloadable music within its various magazines and with corporate products like Coca-Cola.

In theory, one would expect to see competition between different retailers, online ventures and music labels. However Dan Hart, the chief executive of Echo expected the "pressures facing all parts of the music businesses – including distributors, retailers and recording companies – to motivate them all to work together to find a viable alternative to piracy" (Holson 2003c). However, retailers appear to be in a tough spot and will need to work with the labels on the labels' terms given they are trying to by-pass traditional retail methods in order to increase revenue. Plans to sell music online may save some larger chain stores, but the results of this move on independent retail stores may drive them out of business even more in the years ahead. Nonetheless, according to an industry executive, "This [move online] will strategically position retailers to participate in the industry's legitimate downloading future" (Holson 2003b). Ultimately, when content and production companies own or have joint ventures with distribution or retail outlets, the co-called competitive nature of capitalism becomes compromised, which can adversely affect consumer relationships through price increases.

Ultimately, the logic behind the entry into the online market was to move consumers away from hardcopy purchases, as well as scare them away from "illegal" file sharing services in order to corral them into a more regulated environment. The Big 4 can survey consumers, better enforce digital rights management, reduce music copying and eventually earn more money from sales and subscription services. In this new digital world of music commerce, the labels control or regulate nearly every aspect of music creation, from production and distribution, to methods of consumption. The music industry not only increases profits through cheaper manufacturing costs and by cutting out retail, but also by promoting and creating demand for computer hardware and portable music players. Unfortunately, consumers interested in purchasing digital music over the Internet may have to subscribe to several services to access a wide range of music on different labels. The strategy also appears to lock consumers into a service by providing unique abilities that other services do not offer while simultaneously forcing consumers to purchase hardware that may only be compatible with specific music services. It will force consumers into spending more money for music than what they previously spent during vinyl or CD periods.

CONCLUSION

This chapter focused on the music industry's transition into online distribution and its effects on consumers' access to music. It examined the connections the Big 4 are making with ISPs, Web sites that offer music downloads for sale, as well as with hardware and software manufacturing companies. In essence the Big 4 are creating the architecture for online music sales through a tiered system of online music subscription services that offer limited ownership of music. The Big 4's entry into online sales also appears to be harming traditional retail stores. As a result, the race between retail and the Big 4 is to establish online name recognition and/or ownership of various Internet providers and online ventures. Because of these recent trends, this chapter argued the Big 4's transition into digital music sales is giving the music industry more control over online music, more profits when compared with hardcopy formats, as well as more revenue as it begins to take away profits away from retail. As a result, consumers will be forced into buying a number of different services in order to have access and purchase music. Therefore, the music industry is creating a divide between consumers who have enough money to pay for various subscription services and overpriced digital downloads, from those who cannot afford to have access.

NOTES

1. This is somewhat based on an email I received from a middleman organization that connects musicians with online distributors for my own music. I replaced references to the name of the distributor, as well as any dollar amounts with "XXX."

> Got some mildly bad news. Sorry to say, but some digital distribution sales from XXX were double-reported, double-paid, then corrected. All these were sales XXX reported as taking place on May 6 of this year. In getting rid of the duplicates, we had to subtract $XXX from your balance today. It might seem like a lot now, but just think of what the NEXT round of XXX sales will bring in. If you have any questions, please feel free to email me back and ask.

CHAPTER 9

WIRELESS GOLD RUSH

"With over 2 billion mobile devices active worldwide by 2007 and 140 million wireless data users in the U.S. by 2008, wireless entertainment has the opportunity to be bigger than television, radio and online media."

—John Kilcullen, Billboard president/publisher ("Billboard, CTIA In Mobile Confab Pact" 2005)

The wireless gold rush for music and other media delivery is in the process of working its way out in the United States and around the world. Mobile users are beginning to buy ringtones and ringtunes, which are new media created by the music industry for the wireless market. Ringtones are newer versions/simulations of original compositions created though monophonic and polyphonic tones. Ringtunes, sometimes called master ringtones are more expensive, up to $3.00 for one tune. They consist of the actual songs instead of the computerized melody or simulation. Consumers can purchase ringtones or ringtunes of their favorite music to replace the "ring" on their phones.

In 2004, only five percent of U.S. mobile phone users had downloaded a ringtone, while 70 percent of Japanese users had (Banerjee 2004c). This means there is potential for massive growth in this market. According to the British consulting firm Arc Group, global sales of custom ringtones in 2003 were estimated at $3.2 billion dollars, which was an increase of 40 percent from 2002.

Custom ringtones were the most downloaded items over mobile phones as of 2003. By 2004, ringtone sales were a $4 billion market (Banerjee 2004e). In 2005 Virgin reported that 67 percent of its subscribers had purchased a ringtone from its services according to mobile content tracking firm M:Metrics (Bruno 2005d). Moreover, roughly 50 percent of mobile users aged fifteen to thirty have downloaded a ringtone according to one study conducted by research firm Consect (Banerjee 2004e).

Part of the appeal of distributing music via wireless is that there are so many more subscribers than there are actual stores that sell music. As a result, this market has the potential to be the most profitable source of revenue for the music industry. Because wireless distribution of music is new, the market and industry are only beginning to take shape. What was once uncertain, is now "hot" and largely viewed as a good investment. Eventually video games, movies, television and other content may all come through wireless channels.

In terms of mobile carriers, there are five companies that dominate the U.S. market: Sprint, Verizon, Cingular/AT&T Wireless, T-Mobile, and Nextel. Several independent and Big 4 affiliated companies are moving into the wireless market, which is developing very similar to what online music distribution first looked like. There are a number of players and middlemen involved in distributing music through cellular services. Besides labels, musicians, publishers, and songwriters, there are also wireless carriers, repertoire owners, billing agents, content aggregators, and others involved. Aggregators are middlemen who connect wireless carriers and repertoire owners. Aggregators like BlingTones and Zingy also develop, promote and distribute mobile content through carriers. If history repeats itself, it is extremely likely that the Big 4 or their parent companies will merge with, invest in, or purchase the various middlemen involved in distributing music through wireless carriers.

Sony is already doing this through its Run Tunes, where it develops and distributes its own music to carriers (Banerjee 2004c). Indeed, Sony manufactures cell phones, owns the aggregator that distributes music and owns the publishing rights to a lot of the music it distributes. Therefore, their conglomerate structure enables them to extract money at nearly every level in the present configuration of the wireless market. Virgin owner Sir Richard Branson also owns stakes in his Virgin-affiliated company Virgin Mobile, which is a mobile subscription service, and Virgin Records, which is a group of affiliated record companies. Finally, Vivendi SA, which is UMG's parent company, is also in the mobile phone business. It's Société Française de Radiotéléphonie company has 17 million clients.

These companies are in a good position to create the terms and prices for wireless music distribution. They own content (rights to music), manufacture wireless hardware (mobile phones and other devices), own aggregators (middlemen that develop and distribute music), as well as companies that charge subscription fees to access wireless services. Even if further consolidation does not occur, the music industry will need to establish pricing for new media that favors their interests. It seems as if they have already accomplished this feat, which is identified in this chapter's discussion of oligopolistic pricing.

So far, the trends in the music and wireless distribution market are extensions of the music industry's pre-wireless business plan. The move to distribute music via wireless carriers exhibits a continuation of the division of music by label, timing and exclusive content. There is also a continuation of subscription fees, where one has to pay to subscribe to access music before one can purchase the music. In addition, this new platform is characterized by oligopolistic pricing, which increases the profit rate of new media compared to previous media. Last, the continuation of the lock and key strategy, where the purchase of certain media will contain information that will unlock additional information or media through a different medium or subscription service also exists in the wireless market. This strategy continues to force consumers into purchasing different media, hardware, or services in order to access music. Unfortunately, the development of the wireless market and its music distribution infrastructure appear to be created without, or with very little input from consumers and musicians.

EXCLUSIVES

Similar to Internet subscription services, almost every wireless carrier now offers exclusive content. Cingular Wireless has an exclusive 30-second master ringtone from Gwen Stefani's "Hollaback Girl" single ("Bits & Briefs" 2005b). Sprint also offers select songs from UMG and WMG catalogs (Hay 2004a). In addition, BlingTones indicated it would offer exclusive ringtones for a number of wireless carriers. These ringtones were to consist of 30-second mini songs created by some of hip-hops hottest producers such as Q-Tip, Rockwilder, and Hi-Tek (Bruno 2005a). Their service and thus their content, was only supported though Cingular, T-Mobile, and Sprint. Rap star 50 Cent also signed a deal with Zingy to distribute a ringtone service that carried original voice recordings and images. Zingy noted it signed a similar deal with Snoop Dogg (Leeds 2004a).

Virgin Mobile USA is also creating master ringtone exclusives though a deal with UMG (Banerjee 2004d). Virgin Mobile continues to work with MTV for exclusive wireless content, which includes videos (Banerjee 2004d). It recently partnered with UMG to launch the "First Dibs" master ringtone service, which offers exclusive master ringtones from Shady/Interscope artists (Banerjee 2004e). Finally, most latin music ringtones are available through AT&T Wireless, whose catalog comprises of works from EMI, Warner/Chappell, Sony, and Peermusic (Cobo 2004).

Besides music, videos are also beginning to be distributed exclusively through wireless services. For example, the video of the single "I like your records" by the band Super Smart is also only available through mobile phones. The band made the first ringtone album worldwide called "Panda Babies," which sold more than 42,000 times in Europe and the U.S. during the first four months of its release ("Super Smart Ringtone" 2004). In addition, Sprint was the first to offer a broadcast stream of R&B music videos through California Music Channel (CMC) Beat Lounge, country music videos through CMC-USA and international and independent music videos through Independent Music Network. These video options came through a service called MobiTV and initially cost subscribers an additional $15.00 on top of their cellular service (Christman 2004a).

Hardware is also enabling exclusive access to content. Musical artists are creating their own designed mobile phones, which are likely to include games, wallpaper and ringtones based on their creators. Rap superstar 50 Cent was working on his G-Mobile phone in 2005, which was to exclusively include these additions (Bruno 2005c). Sony Ericsson also makes mobile phones. It's K300i phone, valued at roughly $143 in 2005, contained exclusive Faithless downloads and other content. More exclusive Faithless content was available at wireless operator Orange's Orange World online portal (Koranteng 2005b). Faithless is a Sony BMG/Cheeky Records artist. By releasing exclusive musical content from it's music division in the phones it manufactures, Sony was able to use its conglomerate holdings to cross-promote its own content.

The industry's business plan for wireless distribution also relies on timing to generate sales. Indeed, the hope is to create "2 sales" through the release of exclusive music through wireless services before the hardcopy or Internet version is released. For example, Sprint won a two-week distribution deal with Arista Nashville/RCA country act Brooks and Dunn to exclusively allow its subscribers with the ability to download their new single before its release in stores, on the radio, or in hardcopy format ("Bits & Briefs" 2005a).

Besides exclusives and timing, the industry is also using a "lock and key" strategy to increase sales by forcing consumers into purchasing additional hardware or subscription services to access music. For example, mobile phone plans include having stickers on hardcopy CDs in retail stores. After the consumer purchases the CD, he or she could then use his or her cell phone to text in a special code from the sticker on the CD, which would then provide access to exclusive text and content from the artist. The mobile user would be charged a few dollars for the additional transaction (McClure 2003). Here, like the other hardware features discussed in this book, consumers need to purchase a mobile phone, a service, a CD, then pay extra in order to get an exclusive picture, text or song of one of their favorite artists.

OLIGOPOLY DECIDES VALUE AND PRICING

The music industry has also been able to set rates for new media during its transition into wireless distribution. These rates provide the industry with higher profit margins compared to previous media such as cassettes, records or CDs. The oligopolistic pricing is most evident in ringtones and ringtunes. Sony BMG

Music Entertainment, BMG Publishing, EMI Music Publishing, Warner/Chappell Music and Universal Music Group have made deals with each other concerning master ringtones, DualDiscs, Videos and digital rights (Garrity 2005e). EMI music publishing and Sony BMG Music Entertainment formed an agreement on December 17th, 2004 for master ringtones, ringbacks and other digital delivery possibilities, while Warner/Chappell Music Publishing and Warner Music group also formed an alliance around this time (Bruno 2005b). The labels argued they didn't have to follow the traditional mechanical licensing rate that dictates their CD and digital download royalties with these newer digital formats. They decided ringtunes would run between $1.50 and $3.00. Ironically the cost to manufacture a single master ringtone is close to nothing (excluding recording costs), while manufacturing a CD with over ten songs runs around one dollar. Yet, a master ringtone can be sold for three dollars. They are also more costly than digital downloads over the Internet, yet they are essentially the same thing, just that they travel through a different medium. Instead of competing with each other, the "rival" labels and publishers now work together to create newer distribution formats and set prices without any input from the public or musicians (Garrity 2005b).

TRICKLE UP PROFITS

Mobile phone companies license actual recordings from music publishers, paying a 10-12 percent royalty on average for the monophonic or polyphonic tone melody. When the real recording is used, which again is referred to as a "master tone," record labels usually receive a 50 percent cut (Leeds 2004a). If ringtones are defined as licenses, then artists and labels are entitled to a 50-50 split of the profits. If ringtones are defined as a sale, then labels give the contractual royalty to the artist, which gives artists a much smaller percentage of the sale. Estimates are between 6 to 15 percent. There is a move by the labels to define the purchase of legal downloads as sales, which will give the music industry more money (Banerjee 2004b). Sales only require the payment of mechanical and performance royalties to publishing rights holders.

Major wireless carriers keep 10-40 percent of gross revenue from wireless downloads (Banerjee 2004c). Aggregators receive 35-65 percent of retail for polyphonic ringtones and they usually pay the publishing share. With master ringtones they only make 15-20 percent and sometimes even less. The labels want more money from master ringtones and ask for 50 percent of retail, which they would then include the artist cut and maybe the publishing share. Sometimes labels also bypass aggregators and license directly with the carrier as well.

The sale and use of ringtones also requires mechanical and performance fees. Publishers get anywhere between ten cents to 10 percent of the sale for the mechanical rate. Performing rights organizations like BMI and ASCAP ask for 2-2.5 percent of the gross (Banerjee 2004c). According to aggregator Schloeder from Faith West, the master ringtone model is likely to develop into a 40/40/20 split between carriers, repertoire owners and aggregators (Banerjee 2004c).

Although this market is only now taking shape, the companies that own the music industry are beginning to own or invest in each level of this lucrative market. They are likely to maintain their control over music distribution in the wireless market, which continues to make access difficult through exclusives in different services. In addition, the noncompetitive oligopolistic market also created pricing scenarios for new media, which favor the Big 4.

CHAPTER 10

CONCLUSION

The evidence in the previous chapters suggests music is becoming more difficult to access as a result of its division between various services and technologies. At the same time, music is becoming increasingly commercialized and ubiquitous. Conglomerates are spreading out exclusive music through services and technologies because they hope to gain additional revenue through service fees and sales of new technology. The music industry is hoping these changes will counter the recent decline in global music sales, which it blames on consumer file sharing and CD burning. Although file sharing and CD burning may affect the overall value of the music industry, they are not the sole, or even the main causes behind recent sales declines. Several other key influences such as the industry's phasing out of CD singles, the end of the CD replacement cycle, an economic recession, as well as a host of other influences decide industry value.

Besides becoming separated through technology and services, music is also becoming more commercialized and ubiquitous. The industry is increasing advertising and promotion because it benefits from additional revenue and brand awareness. Advertising increases also confront the Internet's potential to empower independent musicians' abilities to circumvent major labels through online distribution networks. These industry changes negatively affect access to culture by creating a divide between those who can afford services fees and new technology and those who cannot. The changes also further blur the line between culture and advertising. In sum, these industry developments are radically altering the manner in which music is accessed, purchased, delivered, and consumed.

While movies, television, video games, and other media are positioned to eventually go through online or wireless distribution channels, the present formation of the music industry should be seen as a pilot project for their development. It is likely that as bandwidth increases, more and more media will require different service fees, hardware, or corporate brands to be accessed. In fact, it is likely that different versions of the same movie, television show or video game may also be dispersed among various services or hardware, which would force consumers into purchasing the same title more than once.

SUMMARY

Looking backward, chapter 2 described the methods used in this investigation, as well as examined theory on new technology and social change. It looked at utopian and dystopian perspectives on media and technology because new technologies are enabling macro shifts within various modes of operation for the music industry. Theory on new technology also provided a general contextualization and framework for the changes occurring in the music industry.

Chapter 3 described the Big 4 companies that manufacture most of the world's music. It also examined conglomeration as related to the music industry, market share, consolidation, recent revenue and ownership patterns. Because the Big 4 are conglomerates, they can easily cross-promote their own content, as well as save money on production costs. Finally, established modes of production resulting from ownership patterns were also investigated. The music industry has been trimming artist rosters, promoting fewer artists, relying on fewer production companies, as well as using new software to determine hit songs. As a result, this chapter argued pop music is becoming less diverse due to industry concentration and pressure to increase revenue.

Chapter 4 focused on the increasing commercial nature of music by industry conglomerates. It noted music companies are using new and more creative methods to market their products, such as co-branding, which has the benefit of streamlining advertising expenditures. The music industry also boosts revenue through royalties and publishing rights when it increases cross-promotion and advertising. As a result of recent increases in music commercialism, this chapter argued the Big 4 are further blurring the line between advertising and culture. In essence, the increase in music commercialism is like an incestuous love affair between and within conglomerates, which turns culture into an advertisement for the corporate media industries.

Chapter 5 continued examining the relationship between conglomeration and culture. Instead of looking at commercialism, it focused on the connections between the Big 4 and various electronics and computer manufacturers. It traced the ownership of CD burners, MP3 players, and video games to the music industry. Finally, this chapter investigated new media such as SACDs and audio DVDs, which the industry hopes will influence additional sales. It argued the music industry hopes to spark multiple sales from one product by combining new hardware and communication services with exclusive music, as well as with the invention of new media forms.

Chapter 6 began the venture into the online world by citing evidence contrary to the argument that file sharing is the main cause behind music industry sales decreases. It argued production-oriented mechanisms such as the trimming of artist rosters, the elimination of CD singles and employee lay-offs influenced the value of the industry between 1999 to 2003. In addition, the economic recession, September 11th attacks, increases in artist, marketing and production costs, the end of the CD-replacement cycle, changing demographics and used CD sales also continue to influence profitability for the Big 4. As a result, even though global sales decreased during 2000–2003, evidence suggests file sharing technology had a minimal impact on industry value, which meant the music industry was nowhere near going bankrupt or out of business.

Chapter 7 continued analyzing new media and technology by focusing on the music industry's response to challenges in copyright infringement resulting from file sharing. It examined "fair use" and its relationship to the debate on file sharing and CD copying. It then described how the music industry has been able to write laws, create new forms of digital rights management technologies, police consumers, as well as manipulate various political platforms in its favor. All of these changes have occurred when recent surveys suggest large numbers of people are not downloading music and that more people are buying MP3 files. This chapter argued the music industry has been using its wealth and political influence to manipulate the legal system in its favor, while using fear of arrest as a means of forcing people into subscribing to "legitimate," or Big 4 supported music services. The result of these developments questioned not only constitutionally protected notions of "fair use," but also the public's ability to operate free from government and private interests in the online world.

Chapter 8 continued examining Internet-related developments by focusing on the music industry's transition into online distribution and its effects on consumers' access to culture. It investigated the connections the Big 4 are making with ISPs, Web sites that offer music downloads for sale, as well as with hardware and software manufacturing companies. These connections increased media consolidation and created a tiered system of online music subscription services that offer limited ownership of music. They are also influencing recent retail store closures, which is sparking retail plans to enter into the online market for music downloads. Because consumers will be forced into buying a number of different services in order to have access and purchase music, this chapter argued the music industry is creating a divide between wealthy consumers who have enough money to pay for various subscription services and overpriced digital downloads, from those who cannot afford to have access.

Finally chapter 9 noted the music industry is continuing its business plan of dividing access to exclusive material throughout different fee-based services

into the wireless market. There is a continuation of the division of music by label, timing, exclusive content, while new lock and key strategies are also being
developed. In addition, this new platform is characterized by oligopolistic pricing while the music industry continues to force consumers into purchasing different media, hardware, or services in order to access music.

THEORETICAL CONTRIBUTION

In terms of contributing to theory on new media and technology, the results of
this investigation support "dystopian" theorists, such as Lessig (1999, 2001,
2005), Shapiro (1999) and Vaidhyanathan (2001, 2004) who suggest people will
be less free to access information and cultural goods in the future. It also supports political and economic theorists such as McChesney (2000b), Schiller
(1999) and Herman and McChesney (1997), who note new technology, such as
the Internet, is more likely to benefit private interests than public interests. It
will also spark more media consolidation while having a minimal negative impact on oligopolistic media markets.

This study also adds a new dimension to the theoretical literature by making
a connection between conglomerate ownership, technology, and access to culture. In the case of the music industry, new media and technology are used as
stimulants to increase sales, which is done by dividing access to various music-
related items through subscription services or new hardware devices, which
must be purchased in order to consume the music. Although the Internet and
wireless technologies are enabling some of these changes, they are not the only
change agents. Additional technologies such as new audio hardware, new media,
as well as technology affiliated with digital rights management are all regulating
how and where consumers experience music. Therefore, the music industry is
using various forms of new technology to enable more control over the distribution and consumption of music, which under their leadership is negatively affecting access to culture.

One must now ask the question, if there is a problem with the music industry, what can be done about it? Consumers have had little to no input in how
they want to experience, pay for, or access music during the transition to online
and wireless distribution of music. The music industry is driving these changes
and does not appear to be looking to alternatives given it has already invested
$2-4 billion dollars in new technological and online initiatives. As a result, con-
sumers are spending more money on music-related expenses than ever before. In
fact, one could even suggest the music industry is punishing people for something they were not responsible for. They do not appear to be the main cause of
decreasing sales, yet they are being forced to make up for them by paying additional service fees and inflated prices for new media. Unfortunately, the media
may not adequately inform the public about these changes since they also stand
to gain due to conglomerate ownership structures. In addition, because the me-

dia work on supply and not demand, most consumers will primarily be exposed to news based on RIAA public relations data, which is designed to push people into purchasing music online or through wireless channels by manufacturing fear of arrest if they download anything outside of the Big 4 subscription services.

WHAT TO DO?

While access to music may not be as important as access to healthcare, education, peace or prosperity, music can move us emotionally, bring people together, as well as make us dance. Moreover, it is important for human development and expression. Given the problems discussed in this book, there are a few proposals that may create a more consumer-friendly and accessible cultural environment.

First, why not make access to healthcare, education and culture a constitutional right, then actually enforce it. At local levels, it may be worth creating resolutions, legislature or amendments that grant the public the right to access not only healthcare and education, but also culture. These grassroots initiatives could eventually expand to impact national documents such as the United States Constitution. Musicians and music fans would need to organize and lobby the U.S. government to change the system in favor of easier access to music, more equitable prices and contracts that also benefit musicians. There are groups already doing this, which have been fairly successful in terms of negotiating better artists' contracts. Other groups such as Creative Commons, Future Music Coalition, Association of Independent Music (AIM) and Free Press are also working to democratize the media and cultural industries.

Unfortunately, government regulation in favor of easier access to music, musical diversity, and affordable prices would probably never happen in the United States unless there was a major social and political revolution that curtailed the influence of private power over the political system. Until this change happens, which may be more likely to occur after a major economic recession (similar to what happened after the great depression), the public should not hold its breath. Nonetheless, other governments around the world may be more likely to listen to the public and create regulation in favor of access and diversity.

Another option is to create a public library for digital music that could be accessed through the Internet or wireless devices. This digital library could allow the public to contribute music, even exclusive music to its content. There would also be a need to create conditions and incentives for labels and musicians in order to build up digital content. For example, in order for a label or musician to obtain a copyright for his or her music, he or she would have to agree to submit it to the digital library. Musicians or labels that would not want to participate would not receive the protection of their music through copyright. This process would begin to build the library's contents, as well as provide the public with access to music, which otherwise may have required them to purchase video game consoles, video game cartridges, and cell phones, as well as additional services.

In order to provide remuneration to musicians and labels that share their music with the library, one possibility could entail considering "checked out" music a public performance. With this definition, the library would then need to register and pay fees to royalty organizations like ASCAP or BMI, which—if well documented—could transfer some money to songwriters and labels. This way, the library could track the movement of music and musicians could still earn some money from their creativity.

Ultimately, in order for the library to work, there would need to be an even debate between musicians, consumers and labels concerning the details of the library's operation. The downloading format, ability to copy, and duration of the "check out" would need to be addressed by musicians, scholars, consumers and labels. Even if these ideas never turn into realities, another alternative is to boycott certain elements of the music industry by supporting artists and labels that do not create exclusive music through a number of services, media and hardware.

Even though this may be an unfair demand for hardcore fans, if no one purchases exclusive music, then the industry may have to change its business plan and allow consumers to directly purchase music without paying subscription fees. It may also force the music industry to move away from separating exclusive music through various hardware and media, which require a number of additional purchases in order to hear the music. Musicians may also want to think twice about participating in the industry's business plan to divide and conquer. Not accepting their business plan may force the music industry into creating a more consumer and culture-friendly approach to music distribution. In fact, boycotting major label music could turn out to be fun for consumers. They could be exposed to a world of new, unique and exciting kinds of music, which rarely register through the conglomerate media. Hopefully some of these ideas will aid in creating a more democratic and egalitarian cultural playing field.

BIBLIOGRAPHY

"1999 World Soundcarrier Sales Flat in Real Terms, up 6 Percent in $." 2000. *Music and Copyright* 176 (February 16).

Ahrens, Frank. 2004. "FTC Approves Sony-BMG; Merger Already Won Go Ahead From E.U. " *Washington Post* (July 20): E, 5.

Alderman, J. 2001. *Sonic Boom: Napster, MP3, and New Pioneers of Music.* Cambridge, Massachusetts: Perseus Publishing.

"Another 'Idol' Hit." 2004. *Billboard* (July 17): 49.

Appelbaum, R.P. and G. Gereffi. 1994. "Power and Profits in the Apparel Commodity Chain." In *Global Production: The Apparel Industry in the Pacific Rim,* ed. E. Bonacich et al. 42–64. Philadelphia, PA: Temple University Press.

"Apple's Online Music Coup Ignites a Budding Industry." 2003. *www.cnn.com/2003/TECH/05/11/apple.online.music.ap/index.htm.* (accessed October 15, 2003).

Association for Progressive Communications. 1997. *Global Networking for Change.* London: Association for Progressive Communications Women's Networking Support Program.

Bachelor, B. 2003. "Music Industry Keeps Its Eye on the Ball." *Billboard* (March 8): 50.

Bagdikian, Ben. 1992. *The Media Monopoly.* Boston, MA: Beacon Press.

Banerjee, Scott. 2004a. "Labels Peer at Pirates for Insights" *Billboard* (April 24): 1, 73.

———. 2004b. "Getting Their Cut." *Billboard* (May 22): 61.

———. 2004c. "Ringtone Rumble Brewing." *Billboard* (May 22): 1, 61.

———. 2004d. "Virgin Rings Up UMG Deal." *Billboard* (June 12): 6.

———. 2004e. "Who'll Drive U.S. Ringtones Market?" *Billboard* (September 18): 3, 76.

———. 2004f. "New Label is Strictly Digital." *Billboard* (October 16): 8.

Banks, J. 1996. *Monopoly Television.* Boulder, Colorado: Westview Press, Inc.

Bartels, Chuck. 2003. "Wal-Mart Starts Test of Online Music Offering." *Atlanta Journal Constitution* (December 18). Lexis-Nexis.

Bates, Ryan. 2004. "Communication Breakdown: The Recording Industry's Pursuit of the Individual User, A Comparison of U.S. and E.U. Copyright Protections for Internet Music File Sharing." *Journal of International Law and Business* 25, no.1: 229.

Baym, N. 1998. "The Emergence of On-Line Community." In S. Jones, *Cybersociety 2.0 Revisiting Computer-Mediated Communication and Community*, 35–68. Thousand Oaks, California: Sage.

Benz, Mathew. 2001a. "Music Retailers See Sales Decline." *Billboard* (June 23). Expanded Academic ASAP: 1.

———. 2001b. "For Multimedia Giants, Synergy Remains Elusive." *Billboard* (October 30): 78.

———. 2001c. "Universal Reports Improved Cash Flow. *Billboard* (November 10): 67.

———. 2002. "Are Major Labels Positioned To Solve Their Problems?" *Billboard* (March 30). 1(2). Expanded Academic ASAP.

Benz, Matthew, Ed Christman and Brian Garrity. 2003. "Consolidation Seen on Fast Track for Big Five." *Billboard* (March 22): 1, 10.

Bessman, Jim. 1999. "BMG, Showtime Hope Music and Boxing Pack a Promo Punch." *Billboard* (July 10): 57, 60.

———. 2003. "Publishers Seek Greater Film/TV Revenue" *Billboard* (December 13): 37.

———. 2004. "Sticking to the Basics." *Billboard* (June 12): 43.

"Bill Would Jail Internet Song Swappers." 2003. *Cnn.com* (accessed October 15, 2003).

"*Billboard*, CTIA In Mobile Confab Pact." 2005. *Billboard* (June 18): 12.

"Bits & Briefs." 2005a. *Billboard* (June 4): 15.

"Bits & Briefs." 2005b. *Billboard* (June 18): 17.

"BMG Entertainment Group." (2003). Hoover's Company Database.

"BMI Reports Record Revenues And Royalty Payments For FY2004." *Music Industry News*. 2004. *www.mi2n.com* in Business News (accessed August 31, 2004).

Bourdieu, Pierre. 1993. *The Field of Cultural Production*. Cambridge, MA: Polity Press.

Brandle, Lars. 2005. "EMI Downloads Optimism" *Billboard* (June 4): 5.

Bruno, Antony. 2005a. "Newsline" *Billboard* (January 8): 8.

———. 2005b. "Wireless Biz Ironing Out Music Kinks." *Billboard* (January 15): 39.

———. 2005c. "G-Unit Adding G-Mobile Unit For Phone and Games, 50 Cent-Style." *Billboard* (May 28): 15.

———. 2005d. "MVNOs Offer Branded Wireless Networks" *Billboard* (June 11): 24.

———. 2005e. "Brands Go Mobile." *Billboard* (June 18): 37, 40.

Bruno, Antony and Brian Garrity. 2005. "Portal Power" *Billboard* (July 2): 22–3.

Buck, Tobias and Tim Burt. 2004. "Brussels Gives Nod to Sony BMG Recorded Music. " *The Financial Times Limited* (July 20): 26.

Burnett, Robert. 1996. *The Global Jukebox: The International Music Industry*. London, UK: Routledge.

Butler, Susan. 2005a. "The Art of the Deal: 2005" *Billboard* (January 8): 1, 61.

———. 2005b. "Royalty Distribution, Accounting Never Easy" *Billboard* (March 2): 49, 61.

Campbell, Richard. 2000. *Media and Culture: An Introduction to Mass Communication*. 2d ed. New York, NY: St. Martin's Press. 93.

Carlozo, L. 2001. "Sounding Off About Music, the Web Conference Corrals Disparate Groups to Debate Future of Art Forum." *Chicago Tribune* (January 11). Lexis-Nexis.

Carter, B. 2003. "Deal May Raise Napster From Online Ashes." *New York Times* (May 19): C1–7.

"CD Technology is a Winner With Consumers." (2003). *Music Industry News Network.* www.mi2n.com (accessed October 15, 2003).

Christman, Ed. 1999. "Retailers Seek Level Playing Field With Net Sales." *Billboard* (November 13): 5–6.

———. 2000a. "Virgin, EMI, Liquid Shine on Harper Web Promo." *Billboard* (May 6): 70.

———. 2000b. "Labels' Actions Could Hurt Business in the Long Run." *Billboard* (May 20): 94.

———. 2000c. "Warner Announces Download Plan." *Billboard* (September 23): 12–13.

———. 2001a. "The Face of the Industry as 2001 Unfolds: Album Sales Increase by Only 4 Percent in 2000." *Billboard* (January 13). Expanded Academic ASAP.

———. 2001b. "SoundScan Numbers Show .35 Percent of Albums Account for More Than Half of All Units Sold." *Billboard* (April 28): 66.

———. 2002. "Labels Ponder Impact of Discounters" *Billboard* (August 31). Expanded Academic ASAP.

———. 2003a. "Retail Health Report: Between Frisco and Florida, What's Changed?" *Billboard* (March 22). Expanded Academic ASAP.

———. 2003b. "Average Sale of Albums Dropped in '02 As Labels Released More, Sold Less." *Billboard* (April 26): 9.

———. 2004a. "Coming Soon To Your Cell Phone: Just About Everything." *Billboard* (January 10): 37.

———. 2004b. "Relatively Speaking, Retail is Rebounding." *Billboard* (January 10): 39.

———. 2004c. "Inside Bronfman's Deal For WMG." *Billboard* (May 29): 1, 76.

———. 2005. "Numbers Look Up for U.S. Biz." *Billboard* (January 15): 5, 59.

Clark, L.S. 1998. "Dating on the Net: Teens and the Rise of 'Pure' Relationships", in *Cybersociety 2.0: Revisiting Computer-Mediated Communication and Community*, ed. S.G. Jones. 159–83. Thousand Oaks, CA: Sage.

Clark, Nicola. 2004. "European Labels Hope Piracy Succumbs to Digital Services." *New York Times* (June 21): C9.

Cobo, L. 2004. "AT&T Wireless Offers Latin Mobile Content" *Billboard* (January 10): 6.

Coleman, S. 1999. "The New Media and Democratic Politics." *New Media & Society*, 1, no. 1: 67–74.

"Compressed Audio Player Market Will Continue To Surge Ahead As Consumers Snap Up Diverse Array Of Devices, Says IDC." 2003. *Music Industry News Network.* www.mi2n.com/press.php3?press_nb=53216 (accessed October 15, 2003).

Conniff, Tamara. 2004. "Sony Music-BMG Merger Sails Through FTC Review." www.hollywoodreporter.com/thr/article_display.jsp?vnu_content_id=1000588987 (accessed August 21, 2006).

Croteau, David and William Hoynes. 2000. *Media/Society: Industries, Images and Audiences*. Thousand Oaks, California: Pine Forge Press.

Danet, B. 1998. "Text as Mask: Gender, Play, and Performance on the Internet." In *Cybersociety 2.0 Revisiting Computer-Mediated Communication and Community*, ed. S. Jones. 129–58. Thousand Oaks, California: Sage.

"Data provided to NYT. " 2003. *New York Times* (April 28): C5.

"Death of the Disc? Music Industry Hopes Over-40 Set's Buying Power Will Keep CDs Viable." 2003. *Janesville Gazette* (April 24): 5–16.

"Declining Music Sales; It's Not All Digital Downloading, Says the NPD Group." 2003. *Music Industry News Network.* www.mi2n.com (accessed October 27, 2003): 1.

Denzin, N. and Y. Lincoln. 1998. "Introduction: Entering the Field of Qualitative Research." In N. Denzin and Y. Lincoln, *Strategies of Qualitative Inquiry*, 1–34. California: Sage.

Dolfsma, W. 2000. "How Will the Music Industry Weather the Globalization Storm?" *Peer Reviewed Journal on the Internet. www.firstmonday.dk/issues/issue5_5/dolfsma/* (accessed October 15, 2003).

Dominick, J. 2002. *The Dynamics of Mass Communication* 6th ed. Boston, MA: McGraw-Hill.

"EFF On College Student Settlements." 2003. *Music Industry News Network. www.mi2n.com* (accessed October 15, 2003).

Einhart, N. 2003. "Who Gets What, The MP3 Economy." *www.business2.com/subscribers/articles/mag/0,1640,49,00.html* (accessed October 15, 2003).

Eisenberg, A. 2003. "Instead of a Radio D.J., a Web Server Names That Tune." *New York Times* (January 23): E8.

Electronic Frontier Foundation, 2005. "Electronic Frontier Foundation. The Customer Is Always Wrong: A User's Guide to DRM in Online Music" *www.eff.org/IP/DRM/guide/* (accessed November 18, 2005).

Eliot, M. 1989. *Rockonomics: The Money Behind the Music*. New York, NY: Franklin Watts. 20–1.

"Elvis Fans All Shook Up Over Digital Music Channel Dedicated To The Icon By Musicnow And BMG." 2003. *Music Industry News Network. www.mi2n.com* (accessed October 15, 2003).

EMI Group plc. 2003. *Hoover's Company Database* (Hoover-no 41769).

"FCC Should Probe 'Payola'." 2003. *Billboard* (December 6): 9.

Fenton, B. 2001. "Random Play." *Sound & Vision.* (November).

Fischer, Dana. 1998. "Rumoring Theory and the Internet: A Framework for Analyzing the Grassroots." *Social Science Computer Review* 16 no. 2: 158–68.

Fischer, Dana and Larry Wright. 2001. "On Utopias and Dystopias: Toward an Understanding of the Discourse Surrounding the Internet." *Journal of Computer Mediated Communication*, 6 no. 2.

Fitzpatrick, E. 1999. "Online Retailers, Artists Team For Exclusive Deals." *Billboard* (April 24): 1.

Flynn, L. 2003. "Apple Offers Music Downloads with Unique Pricing." *New York Times* (April 29): C2.

Freedman, Des. 2003. "Managing Pirate Culture: Corporate Response to Peer-to-Peer Networking." *International Journal of Media Management* 5 no. 3: 173–9.

Gallagher, D. 2003. "For the Mix Tape, A Digital Upgrade and Notoriety." *New York Times* (January 30): E1–6.

"Gaming, Music Industries Inch Closer." 2004. *Digital Music News. www.digitalmusicnews.com/results?title=Electronic%20Arts* (accessed November 14, 2005).

Gardiner. 2003. *Newyorknewsday.com. www.nynewsday.com* (accessed October 15, 2003): 1.

Garnham, N. 1981. "Contribution to a Political Economy of Mass Communication." *Mass Communication Review Yearbook* 1: 123–46.

Garrity, Brian. 2001a. "The Face of the Industry as 2001 Unfolds: Music Companies Feel Dotcom Meltdown." *Billboard* (January 13). Expanded Academic ASAP: 92.

———. 2001b. "Napster, CD Burning, Internet Retail are Hot NARM Confab Topics." *Billboard* (March 13). Expanded Academic ASAP: 1.

——. 2001c. "Napster's Status Outside U.S." *Billboard* (April 14): 76.

——. 2001d. "EMI Teams With CD-Burning Software Developer." *Billboard* (June 16). Expanded Academic ASAP.

——. 2001e. "Retailers Scale Back Third-Quarter Projections In Wake of Attacks." *Billboard* (October 27). Expanded Academic ASAP: 53.

——. 2001f. "Online Music Went Legit in 2001." *Billboard* (December 1): 58.

——. 2002a. "Digital Services Need To Offer More Hit Music." *Billboard* (May 4): 48.

——. 2002b. "Macrovision Forms Music Tech Division." *Billboard* (December 21): 41.

——. 2003a. "Microsoft Readies Copy-Protection Technology." *Billboard* (February 1). Expanded Academic ASAP.

——. 2003b. "Seeking Profits at 99 Cents." *Billboard* (July 12). Expanded Academic ASAP.

——. 2003c. "Warner Revs Up Roster With Chevy Deal." *Billboard* (September 6). Expanded Academic ASAP.

——. 2004a. "Steve's Baby: iTunes Turns One Amid The Tumult." *Billboard* (May 1): 1, 76.

——. 2004b. "Spin Buys Spark New Debate." *Billboard* (June 19): 1, 65.

——. 2004c. "Record Stocks Up, Radio Down." *Billboard* (July 10): 3, 83.

——. 2004d. "The Year of the Download." *Billboard* (July 10): 3, 84.

——. 2004e. "UMG + WMG = Accounting Venture." *Billboard* (October, 30): 1, 60.

——. 2005a. "Global, U.S. Music Markets Show Improvement In 2004: RIAA: Shipments Rise." *Billboard* (April 2): 6, 68.

——. 2005b. "New Sony BMG Deal." *Billboard* (April 30): 10.

——. 2005c. "BMG Direct Buys Rival" *Billboard* (May 21): 10.

——. 2005d. "EMI to Test Copy-Protected CDs In U.S., U.K., Other Markets." *Billboard* (June 18): 12.

——. 2005e. "Sony BMG Inks New Pub Deal." *Billboard* (June 25): 7.

Garrity, Brian and Scott Banerjee. 2004. "Subs May Best Downloads." *Billboard* (August 28): 9, 79.

Garrity, Brian and Lars Brandle. 2004. "While Sales Dwindle, Music Stocks Rise." *Billboard* (January 17): 5, 61.

Garrity, Brian, Matthew Benz and Ed Christman. 2002. "CD Pricing, Used Sales Debated: Concerns Rise Over High Retail Profile of Used CDs." *Billboard* (June 8): 1, 83.

Garrity, Brian and Ed Christman. 2002. "A Forum for Views On Singles, CD Prices, Internet." *Billboard* (March 24): 79.

Gayer, Amit and Oz Shy. 2005. "Copyright Enforcement in the Digital Era." *CESifo Economic Studies* 51 no. 2/3: 477–89.

Gillen, M. A. 2000. "Study Touts Music." *Billboard* (July 29): 1–2.

Goldstein, P. 1994. *Copyright's Highway: From Gutenberg to the Celestial Jukebox.* New York: Hill and Wang.

Grebb, M. 2000. "Music Industry Sees Profits in Going Digital." *Billboard* (January 29): 75.

Greenfeld, K. T. 1999. "You've got Music." *Time Magazine* (February 22). Lexis-Nexis: 3.

Hall, R. 2003. "Rap Snacks Help Nurture Hip-Hop Audience." *Billboard* (May 10). Expanded Academic ASAP:1.

Hansell, Saul. 2003. "AOL Offering Music Catalog for Downloads." *New York Times* (February 26): C1–5.

———. 2004a. "Battle of For (And Function) In MP3 Players." *New York Times* (August 4): C1.

———. 2004b. "Yahoo to Buy Online Music Seller for $160 Million" *New York Times* (September 15): C1, C6.

———. 2004c. "Music Sites Ask, 'Why Buy If You Can Rent?" *New York Times* (September 27): C1.

———. 2004d. "Music Channels Move Into Video And Messages Meant For You" *New York Times* (November 8): C1, C4.

Hardy, P. 2000a. "CD Album Growth Pushes World Sales Up 2 Percent in First Half of 2000." *Music and Copyright* 192.

———. 2000b. "Record Industry: Software Hackers Reportedly Succeeded in Removing Anti-Piracy Watermarks." *Music and Copyright* 192 (October 25).

———. 2000c. "Musicland Purchase Gives Best Buy and Wal-Mart a Third of U.S. Music Market." *Music and Copyright* (December 20).

———. 2000d. "Legal: Section 1201(a) of the Digital Millennium Copyright Act Effective in the U.S." *Music and Copyright* 193 (November 8).

———. 2003a. "UMG and BMG Increase Their World Market Shares, but EMI is the Most Profitable Major." *Music and Copyright* (June 11).

———. 2003b. "Legal." *Music and Copyright* 256 (August 6).

———. 2003c. "Record Industry." *Music and Copyright* 256 (August 6).

———. 2003d. "SME Reports a 10 Percent Fall in Sales to $975m and Operating Losses of $50m in Q1 2003–2004." *Music and Copyright* 256 (August 6).

———. 2003e. "Statistics." Music *and Copyright* 256 (August 6).

———. 2003f. "WMG Reports an 8 Percent Increase in Revenues to $1.05bn in the Second Quarter of 2003." *Music and Copyright* 256 (August 6).

———. 2003g. "As BMG and WMG Edge Closer to Merger the Deal Looks Set to Hinge on Regulators' Concerns." *Music and Copyright* 257 (September 3).

Harmon, A. 2003a. "Music Industry Won't Seek Government Aid on Piracy." *New York Times* (January 15): C3.

———. 2003b. "Verizon Ordered to Give Identity of Net Subscriber." *New York Times* (January 22): C1, C4.

———. 2003c. "Recording Industry Goes After Students Over Music Sharing." *New York Times* (April 23). Lexis-Nexis.

———. 2003d. "Music Swappers Get A Message on PC Screens Stop it Now." *New York Times* (April 30): C1.

———. 2003e. "In Fight Over Online Music, Industry Now Offers a Carrot." *New York Times* (June 8): Section 1, 1.

Hay, C. 2002. "Madison Ave. Woos Musicians." *Billboard* (April 20). Expanded Academic ASAP.

Hay, C. 2004a. "Sprint's Music Tunes To Ring With UMG, WMG Songs." *Billboard* (January, 24): 33.

———. 2004b. "More Musicians Grace The Small Screen." *Billboard* (February 7): 56.

Herman, Edward S. and Noam Chomsky. 1988. *Manufacturing Consent: The Political Economy of the Mass Media.* New York, NY: Pantheon Books.

Herman, Edward S. and Robert McChesney. 1997. *Global Media: The New Missionaries of Corporate Capitalism.* London, UK: Cassell.

Holland, Bill. 2000. "Copyright Cos. Boost U.S. Economy Most." *Billboard* (January 15): 76.

———. 2003. "RIAA Picks New Top Privacy Cop." *Billboard* (December 20): 89.

———. 2004. "Artist Orgs To Aid In Royalty Search." *Billboard* (May 15): 1, 83.

Holland, B. and Brian Garrity. 2003. "Music Biz Piracy Gambit Raises Stakes." *Yahoo.com. www.story.news.yahoo.com* (accessed October 15, 2003): 1.

Holloway, L. 2003a. "Music Label Sees Video Games As Way to Promote New Songs." *New York Times* (March 10): C7.

———. 2003b. "U.S. Stardom Eludes British Pop Sensation." *New York Times* (May 19): C1, C4.

Holson, L. 2003a. "Recoding Industry Lobbyist Plans to Leave Her Position." *New York Times* (January 23): C5.

———. 2003b. "Liquid Audio Gets a Buyer For Its Assets. Wal-Mart's Distributor Shifts Industry Tactics." *New York Times* (January 24): C1.

———. 2003c. "Retailers Said to United to Sell Music Online." *New York Times* (January 27): C2.

Holson, L. and L. Holloway. 2003. "Top Music Executive is Leaving Sony." *New York Times* (January 10): C1–5.

Holson, L. and G. Fabrikant. 2003. "Music Industry Braces for a Shift." *New York Times* (January 13): C1–11.

Hong, Seung-Hyun. 2004. "The Effect of Napster on Recorded Music Sales: Evidence from the Consumer Expenditure Survey." Working Paper for Stanford Institute for Economic Policy Research.

Hoovers.com. *Hoover's Company Database.*

Horwitz, Carolyn. 2002. "Secret Service, RIAA Raid N.Y. Pirate Ring." *Billboard* (December 21): 3.

———. 2004. "ASCAP Reports That Revenue Reached An All Time High of $668 Million." *Billboard* (February 21): 8.

"HP Brings Digital Music To The Masses." 2004. Hewlett-Packard Media Fact Sheet. *www.hp.com/hpinfo/newsroom/press_kits/2004/digitalexplaunch/fs_ music.pdf* (accessed November 28, 2005).

Huckman, M. 2003. "Music Business Gets Commercial." *MSNBC. www.msnbc.com/news/875628.asp* (accessed October 15, 2003): 1.

Hull, G. P. 2000. "The Structure of the Recorded Music Industry." In *The Media and Entertainment Industries: Readings in Mass Communications,* A. N. Greco, 76–98. Boston, MA: Allyn & Bacon.

International Federation of Phonographic Industry. IFPI Fact sheets "Internet Piracy." *www.ifpi.org/site—content/press/20040330c.html* (accessed February, 5, 2006).

Jeffrey, Don. 1999. "Multiple Formats Boost US." *Billboard* (February, 27). Expanded Academic ASAP.

"Joint Statement Following a Meeting of Recording Companies and High Tech Industry." 2003. *Music Industry News Network. www.mi2n.com/press.php3?press_nb=51270* (accessed October 15, 2003): 1.

Jones, S. G. 1998. "Information, Internet, and Community: Notes Toward and Understanding of Community in the Information Age." In *Cybersociety 2.0 Revisiting Computer-Mediated Communication and Community,* ed. S. Jones. 1–34. Thousand Oaks, California: Sage.

"Judge: Millions of CD Buyers Owed Money." 2003. CNN. *www.cnn.com* (accessed October 15, 2003).

Keane, J. 1991. *The Media and Democracy.* Cambridge, MA: Blackwell.

Kelley, N. 2002. "Notes on the Political Economy of Black Music." In *R&B Rhythm and Business: The Political Economy of Black Music*, ed. N. Kelley. Akashic Books: New York.

Kirkpatrick, David. 2003a. "AOL Time Warner Warns of Rift With Bertelsmann." *New York Times* (June 12): C1–8.

———. 2003b. "Time Warner Sells Music Unit for $2.6 Billion" *New York Times* (accessed November 25, 2003). Lexis-Nexis.

Klein, Naomi. 2006. "Pay to Be Saved: The Future of Disaster Response." *www.commondreams.org* (accessed August 30, 2006).

Klinkenborg, V. 2003. "Downloading Music Over the Internet Without Feeling Like a Criminal." *New York Times* (June 7): E14.

Koehn, M. 2003. "Music Specialists Online: Seeking Profits at the Intersection of Site and Store." *Billboard* (March 22). Expanded Academic ASAP.

Kolko, B. and E. Reid. 1998. "Dissolution and Fragmentation: Problems in On-Line Communities." In *Cybersociety 2.0 Revisiting Computer-Mediated Communication and Community,* ed. S. Jones. 129–58. Thousand Oaks, California: Sage.

Koranteng, Juliana. 2005a. "Online Sales' Leap Year." *Billboard* (January 29): 6, 44.

———. 2005b. "Brands Go Mobile." *Billboard* (June 8): 34–5.

Korzeniewicz Miguel. 1993. "Commodity Chains ands Marketing Strategies: Nike and the Global Athletic Industry." In *Commodity Chains and Global Capitalism,* ed. G. Gereffi and M. Korzeniewicz. 247–66. Westport, Connecticut: Praeger.

Langenderfer, Jeff and Steven W. Kopp. 2004. "The Digital Technology Revolution and Its Effects on the Market for Copyrighted Works: Is History Repeating Itself?" *Journal of Macromarketing* 24, no. 1: 17–30.

Lannert, J. 1999. "RIAA Aids Police in Piracy Arrests." *Billboard* (November 13): 44.

Lee, M., and Norman Solomon. 1990. *Unreliable Sources.* New York: Lyle Stuart.

Leeds, Jeff. 2003. "Catalog Record Sales Drop 11 Percent." *LA Times.* *www.polarity1.com/pcrr52.html* (accessed October 15, 2003).

———. 2004a. "The Guy From Green Day Says He Has Your Mother on the Cell Phone." *New York Times* (August 18). C1–3.

———. 2004b. "Record Labels Said to Be Next On Spitzer List For Scrutiny." *New York Times* (October 21): C1.

———. 2004c. "Music Industry Is Trying Out New Releases As Digital Only." *New York Times* (November 22): C1, C6.

Legrand, Emmanuel. 2005. "Global, U.S. Music Markets Show Improvement In 2004: IFPI: Declines Are Slowing" *Billboard* (April 2): 6, 68.

Legrand, Emmanuel and Cesco Van Gool. 2005. "IFPI Seeks Dialogue With ISPs" *Billboard* (April 23): 5, 60.

Lessig, Lawrence. 1999. *Code and Other Laws of Cyberspace.* New York, NY: Basic Books.

———. 2001. *The Future of Ideas: The Fate of the Commons in a Connected World.* New York, NY: Random House.

———. 2005. *Free Culture: How Big Media Uses Technology and the Law to Lock Down Culture and Control Creativity. www.lessig.org.*

Levine, Robert. 2004. "Music Labels Look to DVDs as Sales of CDs Decline." *New York Times* (December 27): C4.

Levy, P. 1997. *Collective Intelligence: Humankind's Emerging World in Cyberspace.* New York: Plenum Press.

Lexis-Nexis Database. Directory of Corporate Affiliations-International Company.

Lichtman, I. 1999a. "Global Publishing Figs Show Modest Growth." *Billboard* (July 31): 1.

Liebowitz, Stan. 2005. "Economists Examine File-Sharing and Music Sales." Forthcoming in *The Industrial Organization of Digital Goods and Electronic Markets*. ed. Pietz and Waelbroeck. Cambridge, MA: MIT Press.

"Major Labels Use Artificial Intelligence to Help Determine 'Hitability' of Music." 2003. *www.mi2n.com/press.php3?press_nb=48160* (accessed October 15, 2003).

Mann, C. 2000. The Heavenly Jukebox. *Atlantic Online*. *www.theatlantic.com/cgi-bin/o/issues/2000/09/mann.htm* (accessed October 15, 2003): 53, 56, 59.

Marriott, M. 2003. "Getting Game Boy to Play Their Tune: Lacking Investors but Winning Allies, a Duo Guides a Music Gadget to Market." *New York Times* (February 6): C1, C4.

Masson, G. 2002. "IFPI Reports Global Sales Decline For 2001 Music Shipments." *Billboard* (April 27): 6.

———. 2003. "IFPI: Global Sales Down 7.6 Percent in '02." *Billboard* (April 19): 1.

Mathews, Anna. 2003. "Roxio to Buy Pressplay and Revive Napster Name." *Wall Street Journal* (May 19): B4.

Mazzocco, D. 1994. *Networks of Power*. Boston, MA: South End Press.

McChesney, Robert. 1997. *Corporate Media and the Threat to Democracy*. New York: Seven Stories Press.

———. 1998. "The Political Economy of Global Communication." In *Capitalism and the Information Age: The Political Economy of the Global Communication Revolution*, ed. R. McChesney, E. Wood and J. Foster. 1–26. New York, NY: Monthly Review Press. 4, 8.

———. 2000a. "The Political Economy of Communication and the Future of the Field." *Media Culture and Society*, 22: 109–116.

———. 2000b. *Rich Media, Poor Democracy: Communication Politics in Dubious Times*. Revised ed. Chicago, IL: University of Illinois Press.

McClure, Steve. 2000. "Toshiba-EMI Spurs Group's Results." *Billboard* (June 3): 108.

———. 2003. "Newsline." *Billboard* (November 8): P. 8.

McCormick, M. 2000. "Disney Records Target Tweens With Four Titles." *Billboard* (May 20): 90–1.

McCourt, Tom and Patrick Burkart. 2003. "When Creators, Corporations, and Consumers Collide: Napster and the Development of Online Music Distribution." *Media, Culture and Society*, 25: 333–50.

McQuail, D. 1994. *Mass Communication Theory: An Introduction*. London, UK: Sage.

Meehan, Eileen. 2005. *Why TV is not our Fault: Television Programming, Viewers, and Who's Really in Control*. Lanham, Maryland: Rowman & Littlefield.

Mosco, Vincent. 1996. *Political Economy of Communication*. Thousand Oaks, California: Sage.

Murdock, G. and P. Golding. 1979. "Capitalism, Communication and Class Relations." In *Mass Communication and Society*, ed. J. Curran, M. Gurevitch, and J. Woollacott. 12–43. Thousand Oaks, California: Sage.

"Music—Related Dotcoms Hit by the Continuing Online Shakeout." 2001. *Music and Copyright* 197 (January 17).

"Music Slump: 'Worst may be over.'" 2004. Cnn. *www.Cnn.com* (accessed on April 7, 2004).

"Music Stats." 2005. *www.weblogs.usc.edu/ccp/archives/2005/10/music stats.html* (accessed October 5, 2005).

"Napster Gives Away Music Players With Subscription." 2004. Cnn.com (accessed June 17, 2004).

Nelson, C. 2003. "Recalling 45's, Music Labels Push Market for DVD Singles." *New York Times* (April 28): C7.

Newman, Melinda. 2004a. "Atlantic, EMI Pub's Lamberg Bow Label." *Billboard* (April 24): 6, 69.

———. 2004b. "Gray, Cole Sing a Song For Advertisers." *Billboard* (September 4): 13.

———. 2005. "The Last Word" *Billboard* (January 8): 62.

Oberholzer-Gee, Felix and Koleman Strumpf. 2005. *"The Effect of File Sharing on Record Sales An Empirical Analysis. Working Paper."* www.unc.edu/~cigar/strumab.htm (accessed December 1, 2005).

Office of Technology Assessment. 1989. *Copyright and Home Copying: Technology Challenges the Law* (OTA Publication No. CIT-422). Washington, DC: U.S. Government Printing Office.

Olson, C. A. 1999a. "Yahoo! To Sell Downloads." *Billboard* (September 4): 6–7.

———. 1999b. "Musicmaker.com Lands Big Acts in Deal." *Billboard* (September 11): 82–3.

"Partnership to Securely Distribute Digital Music." 2003. *Music Industry News Network.* www.mi2n.com (accessed October 15, 2003).

Passman, D. 2003. "The Digital Tunnel Will Yield Light." *Billboard* (June 21). Expanded Academic ASAP.

Pavlik, J. 1998. *New Media Technology: Cultural and Commercial Perspectives.* 2d ed. Needham Heights, MA: Allyn and Bacon.

Peitz, Martin and Patrick Waelbroek. 2004. "The Effect of Internet Piracy on Music Sales: Cross-Section Evidence." *Review of Economic Research on Copyright Issues* 1 no. 2: 71–9.

Peterson, R. A. and D. G. Berger. 1990. "Cycles in Symbol Production: The Case of Popular Music 1975." In *On Record: Rock, Pop & the Written Word*, ed. S. Frith and A. Goodwin. 140–59. New York, NY: Pantheon Books.

Pew Internet & American Life Project. (2000). "Downloading Free Music: Internet Music Lovers Don't Think it's Stealing." www.pewinternet.org (accessed October 15, 2003).

Pham, A., and P. J. Huffstutter. 2003. "Sony Unveils PSX Console." *Los Angeles Times* (May 29): C1, C11.

"Pirate CD Sales Top 1 Billion." 2003. *CNN.com.* www.editionl.cnn.com (accessed October 15, 2003).

Pogue, D. 2003. "The Internet As Jukebox, At a Price." *New York Times* (March 6): C1, C6.

Pohlmann, K. 2001. "My Moral Dilemma." *Sound & Vision* (November).

Poster, M. 1997. "Cyberdemocracy: The Internet and the Public Sphere." In *Virtual Politics: Identity & Community in Cyberspace*, ed. D. Holmes. 212–29. London, UK: Sage.

"Pressplay Becomes First Music Service to Include J Records in its Catalog." 2003. *Music Industry News Network.* www.mi2n.com (accessed October 15, 2003).

Pride, D. 1999. "Hitmaking Teams Expand Control." *Billboard* (December 18): 1.

"Promo Uses CDs in Soft Drink Cup Caps." 2003. *Cincinnati Enquirer.* www.enquirer.com/editions/2003/07/02/biz_cdmarketing02.html (accessed July 28, 2003).

"Race To Merge Picks Up Pace." 2003. *Billboard* (November 1): 9.

Ralis, D. 2003. "Stop of I'll Sue." *Burlington County Times. www.phillyBurbs.com* (accessed October 15, 2003).

"Rap, Dance/Club and Alternative Rock Most Popular With Online Music Downloaders." 2003. *Music Industry News Network. www.mi2n.com/press.php3?press_nb=51541* (accessed October 15, 2003).

"Record Labels Send ISPs Subpoenas in Piracy Battle." 2003. *CNN. www.cnn.com* (accessed October 15, 2003): 1.

Recording Industry Association of America (RIAA). *www.riaa.com.*

"Revealed: How RIAA Tracks Downloaders, Music Industry Discloses Some Methods Used." 2003. *CNN. www.cnn.com* (accessed October 15, 2003).

Rheingold, Howard. 1993. *The Virtual Community: Homestead on the Electronic Frontier.* New York, NY: Harper Perennial.

"RIAA Brings New Round of Illegal File Sharing Lawsuits." 2004. *Music Industry News Network. www.mi2n.com/press.php3?press_nb=70592* (accessed August, 26, 2004).

"RIAA Steps Up Effort Against Illegal File Sharers, EDonkey Users Among Those Sued." 2004. *Music Industry News Network. www.mi2n.com* (accessed August 31, 2004).

"RIAA Sues 532 More Over Online Swapping." 2004. *msnbc.com. www.msnbc.msn.com/id/4587120/* (accessed March 23, 2004).

Richtel, M. 2003. "Apple is Said to be Entering E-Music Fray With Pay Service." *New York Times* (April 28): C1, C2, C5.

Roberts, Michael. 2002. "Big Music's Post-Fordist Regime and the Role of Independent Labels." In *R&B Rhythm and Business: The Political Economy of Black Music.* ed. N. Kelley. Akashic Books: New York. 28, 32, 34–5.

Robischon, Noah. 2004. "Hey, Cool Music. And There's a Video Game, Too?" *New York Times* (November 15): C1.

Rothman, W. 2003. "Beyond the CD: A Bid to Burmish Records' Sheen: Besieged on One Digital Front, the Industry Looks to Another to Restore Music's Price Tag." *New York Times* (March 13): E1, E7.

Schiller, Daniel. 1999. *Digital Capitalism: Networking the Global Market System.* Cambridge, MA: Massachusetts Institute of Technology.

Schwartz, John. 2004. "A Heretical View of File Sharing." *New York Times* (April 5): C1, C4.

Seay, D. 2000. "The Hottest Sector of the Promotional-Music Market: Publishing and Goods-Publishing." *Billboard* (May 20): S4.

"Self-Destruct Files to Secure DVDs, CDs." 2003. *CNN. www.cnn.com/2003/TECH/internet/06/17/copyright.rdm.reut/index.html* (accessed October 15, 2003).

"Senator: Trash Illegal Downloaders' Pcs." 2003. CNN. *www.cnn.com* (accessed June 18, 2003).

Shapiro, A. L. 1999. *The Control Revolution: How the Internet is Putting Individuals in Charge and Changing the World We Know.* New York: Public Affairs.

Shatz, T. 1997. "Return of the Hollywood Studio System." In *Conglomerates and the Media.* ed. Erik Barnouw. 73–106. New York: The New York Press.

Shuker, R. 2001. *Understanding Popular Music.* New York: Routledge. 29,39.

"Sites + Sounds Newsline." 2002. *Billboard* (December 14): 40.

"Sony/Microsoft and UMG/AT&T Form Digital Delivery Alliances." 1999. *Music and Copyright* 159 (May 19).

"Sony Music Entertainment Inc." 2003. *Hoover's Company Database* (Hoover-no 56304).

"Sony Music Nashville Slashes Artist Roster." 2003. *Billboard* (June 13). Expanded Academic ASAP.

"Sony Music-BMG Merger Sails Through FTC Review." 2004. *www.Thehollywoodreporter.com* (accessed July 29, 2004).

Stanton, Mark W. 2005. "Research in Action Issue 17. Employer-Sponsored Health Insurance: Trends in Cost and Access." *www.ahrq.gov/research/empspria/empspria.htm* (accessed November 21, 2005).

Stark, Phyllis. 2004. "Digital Dissonance." *Billboard* (July 10): 3.

Stevens, Lonnie and David Sessions. 2005. "An Empirical investigation into the Effect of Music Downloading on the Consumer Expenditure of Recorded Music: A Time Series Approach." *Journal of Consumer Policy*, 28 no. 3: 311–24.

Strauss, N. 2003. "Computer Hits." *New York Times* (March 12): B3.

Sunstein, C. 2001. *Republic.com*. Princeton, NJ: Princeton University Press.

"Super Smart Ringtone-Albums: Sales Figures Beat The Records." 2004. *www.mi2n.com* (accessed August, 16, 2004).

Tagliabue, J. 2003. "Vivendi Posts $25 Billion Loss; Will Explore Shedding Assets." *New York Times* (March 7): C1, C6.

Tambini, D. 1999. "New Media and Democracy." *New Media & Society*, 1 no. 3: 305–29.

Taylor, C. 2001. "Preteens a Lucrative, if Vulnerable, Market." *Billboard* (May 12): 1–2.

———. 2003. "Celine Tries New Marketing Road, Sponsor Tie-ins, Vegas Shows Drive Promotion Strategy." *Billboard* (March 22): 1, 24.

"The Next Generation Cracking Defense SecuROM By Sony DADC Takes Copy Protection to a New Level." 2003. *Music Industry News Network. www.mi2n.com* (accessed October 15, 2003).

"The Rolling Stones' Music Available In Legitimate Digital Format For First Time Via RealNetworks' Rhapsody And Best Buy Exclusive." 2003. *Music Industry News Network. www.mi2n.com* (accessed October 15, 2003).

Timmons, Heather. 2004. "EMI to Cut Artist Roster And Close 2 CD Plants." *New York Times* (April 1): W1.

"Tracking." 2001. *Music and Copyright* 198 (January 31).

Traiman, Steve. 1999a. "Music Goes To The Movies." *Billboard* (January 9): 6.

———. 1999b. "More Musicians Explore Video Game Work." *Billboard* (June 5): 101.

———. 1999c. "More Music-Related Projects Using Merchandise Licensing." *Billboard* (July 3): 63.

———. 2001a. "As the Gaming World Grows, So Do Music Opportunities." *Billboard* (June 9). Expanded Academic ASAP.

———. 2001b. "Riese, HMV Try Marketing Music Where Customers Eat." *Billboard* (September 8). Expanded Academic ASAP.

———. 2001c. "Video Games Provide New Platform For Music Promotion." *Billboard* (December 8). Expanded Academic ASAP.

———. 2003a. "Brand Licensing and Merchandise." *Billboard* (June 14): 21.

———. 2003b. "For Sony Games Arm, It's PS2, I Love You." *Billboard* (November 15): 60.

———. 2004a. "Music, Games Tightened Their Commercial Bond" *Billboard* (January 10): 41, 46.

———. 2004b. "NFL Title Kicks Off Deal" *Billboard* (January 17): 38.

Tsagarousianou, R. 1998. "Electronic Democracy and the Public Sphere: Opportunities and Challenges." In *Cyberdemocracy: Technology, Cities and Civic Networks*, ed. R. Tsagarousianou, D. Tambini and C. Bryan. 167–78. London, UK: Routledge.

Turow, J. 1997. *Breaking up America: Advertisers and the New Media World.* Chicago, IL: University of Chicago Press.

"Ubi Soft Entertainment Signs Musician/Actress Eve to Voice Highly Anticipated Videogame - XIII." 2003. *Music Industry News Network. www.mi2n.com* (accessed 15, 2003).

"Universal Music Group." 2003. *Hoover's Company Database* (Hoover-no 100557).

"U.S. Copyright Office Report Might Extend First Sale Doctrine to Digital Downloads." 2001. *Music and Copyright* 199 (February 14).

U.S. Department of Education. 2004. "Special Analysis 2004: Paying for Colleges Between 1990 and 2000 for Full-Times, Dependent Undergraduates." Institute of Educational Sciences. *http://nces.ed.gov/programs/coe/2004/analysis/index.asp* (accessed August 12, 2006).

U.S. International Trade Commission Third Annual Report. 2002. *U.S. Trade and Investment with Sub-Saharan Africa.* TSITC Publication No. 3552. Washington, DC: U.S. Government Printing Office.

"U.S. Slowdown Points to 2 Percent Fall in Value of Global Soundcarrier Sales." 2001. *Music and Copyright* 198 (January 31).

Vaidhyanathan, Siva. 2001. *Copyrights and Copywrongs: The Rise of Intellectual Property and How it Threatens Creativity.* New York: New York University Press. 27.

———. 2004. *The Anarchist in the Library: How the Clash Between Freedom and Control is Hacking the Real World and Crashing the System.* New York: Basic Books.

Veiga, A. 2003. "Artists Embrace Mobile Music Promotions." *Associated Press in The Australian* (June 17). Lexis-Nexis database: C2.

Viera, Miguel Said. 2003. "Property and Copyright: From Herculano to Vaidhyanathan: A Brazilian Perspective." *Publishing Research Quarterly* 19, no. 3: 21–5.

Vogel, H. 1994. *Entertainment Industry Economics: A Guide to Financial Analysis.* 3d ed. New York: Cambridge University Press.

———. 2001. *Entertainment Industry Economics.* 5 ed. New York: Cambridge University Press. 148.

Vogel, Richard. 2006. "Harder Times: Undocumented Workers and the U.S. Informational Economy" Monthly Review 58, no. 3: 29–39.

"Wal-Mart Tunes Up Online Music Store." 2004. *M S N B C. www.msnbc.msn.com/id/4585458* (accessed March 23, 2004).

Walsh, Christopher. 2001. "Market Overview: A Year of Living Dangerously?" *Billboard* (March 31): 60.

———. 2002. "How the Music Industry Burns Itself." *Billboard* (March 30). Expanded Academic ASAP.

———. 2004. "Formats Offer Diversity." *Billboard* (May 1): 50.

———. 2005. "DVD Keeps Things Busy." *Billboard* (March 19): 39, 40.

"Warner is Music to EMI's Ears." 2005. *Financial Times.* (February 6). Global News Wire-Asia Africa Intelligence Wire.

"Warner Music Group." 2003. *Hoover's Company Database* (Hoover no. 103151).

Wasko, Janet. 1993. Introduction: Studies in Communication Democracy. In *Communication and Democracy,* ed. S. Splichal and J. Wasko. 163–7. Norwood, NJ: Ablex.

"Weaving 'Spider-Man' Music." 2004. *Billboard* (July 3): 7, 69.

Wellman, B. 1997. "The Road to Utopia and Dystopia on the Information Superhighway." *Contemporary Sociology,* 26 no. 4: 445–9.

"Why Experts are Predicting the Imminent Demise of the Modern Music Medium." 2003. *Janesville Gazette* (April 24): 5, 14, 16.

Wilhelm, A. G. 2000. *Democracy in the Digital Age.* New York: Routledge.

"World Soundcarrier Sales Rose 1.5 percent 1999 in Constant Dollars to $3.8BN." 2000. *Music and Copyright* 181 (May 10).

www.fretplay.com. 2006. *www.fretplay.com/tabs/a/aerosmith/walk_this_way- tab.shtml* (accessed July, 9, 2006).

Zentner, Alejandro. 2003. *"Measuring the Effects of Music Downloads on Music Purchases."* University of Chicago. Working Paper. *http://home.uchicago.edu/~alezentn/musicindustrynew* (accessed October 29, 2005).

Index

137

About The Author

David J. Park is an assistant professor at Xavier University of Louisiana. He holds a Ph.D. from the University of Wisconsin-Madison and lives in New Orleans. He has published in the *Global Media Journal, Journal of Critical Inquiry, American Behavioral Scientist,* and other journals. As an independent record label co-owner and musician, he has continued his involvement in the music industry while enduring academia.

www.ingramcontent.com/pod-product-compliance
Lightning Source LLC
Chambersburg PA
CBHW051243050326
40689CB00007B/1047